New
ENTERPRISE

A1

Student's Book

Jenny Dooley

JN125953

Express Publishing

CONTENTS

2

	Grammar	Vocabulary	Reading	Listening	Speaking	Writing	Culture
7 **Taste the world** (pp. 56-63)	• countable/ uncountable nouns • phrases of quantity • *some, any, a lot of/ much/many – how much/how many – a few/a little* • the imperative	• food/drinks • cutlery & tableware • ways to cook • food preparation	*Food of the World* (article – complete sentences)	a restaurant advert (gap fill)	• ordering food • **pronunciation:** /g/ /dʒ/	• a restaurant review **writing tip:** using adjectives	*Traditional Irish Recipes*
8 **New places, new faces** (pp. 64-71)	• comparative – superlative • adverbs of degree *(quite, very, much, too)* • *too/enough*	• adjectives describing places • tourist attractions	*Los Angeles – The City of Angels* (article – T/F statements – answer questions)	a dialogue (multiple matching)	• making suggestions • **pronunciation:** /s/ /ʃ/	• an article about a place **writing tip:** title, tenses, informal language in articles	*Welcome to New Zealand*
9 **Times change** (pp. 72-79)	• past simple *(was/ were, had, could)*	• features in a place • places/ buildings in a town/city • transport	*Inishmore: Then & Now* (article – answer questions)	directions (gap fill)	• asking for/ giving directions • **pronunciation:** /l/ pronounced or silent	• an article about a place then and now **writing tip:** linking ideas: *because/so*	*UK street names*

Values – Respect (p. 80)
Public Speaking Skills C – present a historic landmark (p. 81)

	Grammar	Vocabulary	Reading	Listening	Speaking	Writing	Culture
10 **Their stories live on** (pp. 82-89)	• past simple (regular/ irregular) • prepositions of movement • adverb formation	• famous people and their achievements • jobs • feelings/ reactions	*Making the Best of a bad situation* (article – T/F statements; multiple matching)	a narration of an event (order of events)	• narrating past events • intonation *Yes/ No* questions	• a story **writing tip:** adjectives/ adverbs; join sentences (*and, but, because, so then, when*, etc)	*William Shakespeare – A Poet for All Time*
11 **Time will tell** (pp. 90-97)	• *should/shouldn't* • future simple, *be going to*, present continuous (future meaning) • *It – There*	• the environment • summer plans	*A Dark Future or a Bright One?* (blog – complete sentences)	a dialogue about summer plans (multiple choice)	• giving advice • inviting/ accepting/ refusing invitations • **pronunciation:** *'ll – won't*	• an email about your summer plans **writing tip:** expressing reason, result or purpose	*Arbor Day – Give a Little Time to the Trees*
12 **Take a break** (pp. 98-105)	• present perfect • present perfect vs past simple • *The/–*	• holiday activities • travel experiences	*Exotic Morocco* (email – T/F statements)	telephone conversations (multiple choice)	• describing holiday experiences • **pronunciation:** /h/ pronounced or silent	• a blog comment about a holiday experience **writing tip:** opening/closing remarks	*Adventure Holidays in Canada*

Values – Environmental Awareness (p. 106)
Public Speaking Skills D – present a green city (p. 107)

CLIL (pp. 108-111)
Word List (pp. 112-118)
Irregular Verbs (p. 119)

1

Hi!

Reading

1 Look at the social media profiles. How old is each person? What is their dream job?

🎧 Listen and read to find out.

▼ Peter Smith

▸ **Age:** 16
▸ **Country:** the UK

I'm good at singing. Music is my favourite subject at school. My favourite artist is Bruno Mars. He is an American singer and he can sing really well. My dream job is to become a singer. It's an amazing job.

👍 Likes ▾   🗎 Save   ➤ Share   ⋯ More ▾

▼ Maria Álvarez

▸ **Age:** 18
▸ **Country:** Argentina

I'm really interested in Art and ICT. I can draw beautiful pictures. I can design great outfits on my computer as well. My dream job is to become a fashion designer. It's a great job!

👍 Likes ▾   🗎 Save   ➤ Share   ⋯ More ▾

▼ Ju Luó

▸ **Age:** 19
▸ **Country:** Thailand

I'm crazy about English Literature. My favourite writers are Margaret Atwood, John Steinbeck and Charles Dickens. I can write good stories. My dream job is to become a writer.

👍 Likes ▾   🗎 Save   ➤ Share   ⋯ More ▾

▼ Janusz Florek

▸ **Age:** 20
▸ **Country:** Poland

At my college, all of the subjects are interesting, but my favourite one is Art. I'm mad about photography. I can take really good snapshots with my camera. My dream job is to become a photographer.

👍 Likes ▾   🗎 Save   ➤ Share   ⋯ More ▾

2 Read the sentences. Replace the words in bold with words from the text.

1 Peter is good at **it**.

2 Maria is interested in **them**.

3 **She**'s interested in English Literature.

4 Janusz can take **these** with his camera.

> ✓ **Check these words**
>
> good at, become, amazing, interested in, draw, design, outfit, crazy about, mad about, snapshot

Speaking

3 a) 🗣️🗣️ **Ask and answer questions, as in the example.**

A: **What** is Peter's surname?

B: Smith.

A: **How old** is he?

B: He's 16 years old.

A: **Where** is he from?

B: He's from the UK.

A: **What** is his dream job?

B: His dream job is to become a singer.

b) **Read the texts again. Copy and complete the table. Make sentences, as in the example.**

First name	Surname	Age	Country	Dream Job
Peter	Smith	16	the UK	singer
Maria	Álvarez			
Ju				
Janusz				

… is … years old. **He/She** *is from … .* **His/Her** *dream job is to become … .*

Vocabulary
Cardinal numbers

4 a) 🎧 **Listen and learn.**

one (1)	eleven (11)	thirty (30)
two (2)	twelve (12)	forty (40)
three (3)	thirteen (13)	fifty (50)
four (4)	fourteen (14)	sixty (60)
five (5)	fifteen (15)	seventy (70)
six (6)	sixteen (16)	eighty (80)
seven (7)	seventeen (17)	ninety (90)
eight (8)	eighteen (18)	a hundred (100)
nine (9)	nineteen (19)	a hundred and one (101)
ten (10)	twenty (20)	a thousand (1000)
	twenty-one (21)	

b) 🎧 **Listen and circle the numbers you hear. Write them in your notebook.**

47 5 3 **67** 13 **28** 96 **56** 100 64 89 34

forty-seven

Countries/Nationalities

5 **Fill in the gaps with words from the list. Write in your notebook. Then make sentences, as in the example.**

- Brazil • Mexican • Argentina
- Japanese • Greek • Spain • Finland
- American • Canada • Turkey

Name	Nationality	Capital	Country
Paolo	Brazilian	Brasilia	**1)** *Brazil*
Pablo	Spanish	Madrid	**2)** ....
Jason	Canadian	Ottawa	**3)** ....
Ito	**4)**	Tokyo	Japan
Tomás	Argentinian	Buenos Aires	**5)** ....
Mike	**6)**	Washington DC	the USA
Costas	**7)**	Athens	Greece
Hans	Finnish	Helsinki	**8)** ....
Rico	**9)**	Mexico City	Mexico
Ali	Turkish	Ankara	**10)** ....

Paolo is Brazilian. He's from Brasilia, Brazil.

Writing

6 **Copy and complete the table in Ex. 3b with information about your friend. Use your notes to write a paragraph about him/her (50 words). Add a photo.**

Grammar in Use

Tony is from London, the UK. He's 18 years old. Tony is good at drawing, but he isn't good at singing. His dream job is to become an architect. He can play football well, but he can't play tennis.

1 Read the table. Find examples in Tony's profile.

The verb *to be*

Affirmative		Negative	
Long form	**Short form**	**Long form**	**Short form**
I am	I'm	I am not	I'm not
you are	you're	you are not	you aren't
he	he's	he	he
she ⎤ is	she's	she ⎤ is not	she ⎤ isn't
it	it's	it	it
we	we're	we	we
you ⎤ are	you're	you ⎤ are not	you ⎤ aren't
they	they're	they	they
Interrogative		**Short answers**	
Am I?		Yes, I am. / No, I'm not.	
Are you?		Yes, you are. / No, you aren't.	
	he?	Yes, he is. / No, he isn't.	
Is	she?	Yes, she is. / No, she isn't.	
	it?	Yes, it is. / No, it isn't.	
	we?	Yes, we are. / No, we aren't.	
Are	you?	Yes, you are. / No, you aren't.	
	they?	Yes, they are. / No, they aren't.	

2 Fill in: *is, are, 's, 're, 'm, aren't* or *isn't*.

1 A: *Is* he from Mexico?
B: No, he .... He .... from Japan.

2 A: .... they Spanish?
B: No, they .... They .... Canadian.

3 A: What .... your favourite school subject?
B: My favourite school subject .... Music.

4 A: .... Paolo from Brazil?
B: Yes, he .... He .... from Brasilia.

5 A: How old .... you?
B: I .... 23.

6 A: .... she from Italy?
B: Yes, she .... She .... from Milan.

3 a) Complete the gaps with the correct form of the verb *to be*.

Hi! My name **1)** *is* Andrea and I **2)** .... from the UK. I **3)** .... 25 years old. This **4)** .... my friend Monica. She **5)** .... from Poland. She **6)** .... 28 years old. We **7)** .... photographers. I **8)** .... good at drawing, and Monica **9)** .... good at singing. In this photo, we **10)** .... at a café. Be our e-friend.

b) Correct the sentences. Write in your notebook.

1 Andrea is from Poland.
Andrea isn't from Poland. She's from the UK.

2 Monica is 25 years old.

3 Andrea and Monica are American.

4 Andrea is a good singer.

4 **SPEAKING** **Pretend you are from one of the countries below. Your partner tries to guess where you are from.**

• Australia • India • Peru • France • Germany
• Bahrain • Portugal • Brazil • Italy • Egypt

A: *Are you from Italy?*
B: *No, I'm not.*

A: *Are you from France?*
B: *Yes, I am.*

5 Read the theory box. Then fill in the correct subject pronoun.

Subject pronouns

Singular	I/You/He/She/It
Plural	We/You/They

Subject pronouns go before the main verb.
John is from Peru. **He** is Peruvian.

1 Mary is from the UK. .... is British.

2 Tom and I are 18 years old. .... are Canadian.

3 Sue and Molly are students. .... are from the USA.

4 I am interested in Art. .... is my favourite subject.

5 Mark is 28 years old. .... is a photographer.

6 You and Anna are from Canada. .... are Canadians.

6 Read the theory. Find one example in Tony's profile on p. 6.

a/an

- We use **a/an** before singular nouns when we talk generally about them. We also use **a/an** before names of jobs. *a book*, *an actor*
- We use **a** before consonant sounds (*b, c, d, f*, etc). *He's a teacher*. We use **an** before vowel sounds (*a, e, i, o, u*). *She's an actress*.

7 **a)** Use *a/an* and the words: *artist, astronaut, doctor, engineer, pilot, police officer, vet, waiter, waitress, actress/actor, secretary* to label the pictures.

Steven (27)

Kathy (26)

1 *a waiter*

2 ....

Mary (30)

Laura (29)

Bob (35)

3 ....

4 ....

5 ....

Helen (34)

Steve (42)

Paul (36)

....

7 ....

8 ....

Stella (28)

Tom (38)

Pam (28)   Peter (30)

....

10 ....

11 ....

b) **SPEAKING** Ask and answer questions about the people in Ex. 7a.

A: **What's** his name?
B: Steven.
A: **How old** is he?
B: Twenty-seven.

A: **What's** his job?
B: He's a waiter.

8 Read the table. Find examples in Tony's profile on p. 6.

The verb *can*

Affirmative	I/You/He/She/It/We/You/They **can**.
Interrogative	**Can** I/you/he/she/it/we/you/they?
Negative	I/You/He/She/It/We/You/They **cannot/can't**.

9 Say what each person *can/can't* do.

1
Mark / cook (✗)

2
Mary / type (✓)

3
Lora / dance (✗)

4
Steve / swim (✓)

5
Sam / play the guitar (✗)

6
Kate / run (✓)

1 Mark can't cook.

10 **SPEAKING** In groups, ask and answer questions to find out what your friends *can* or *can't* do. Use the phrases in the table.

very well/fast	95%	
quite well/fast	70%	
not very well/fast		40%
no		0%

A: Can you cook?
B: Yes, I can cook very well. Can you type?
A: No, I can't. Can you type?
C: Yes, I can type quite well. Can you ... ? etc

7

Skills in Action

Vocabulary
School/College subjects

1 a) 🎧 **Listen and learn.**

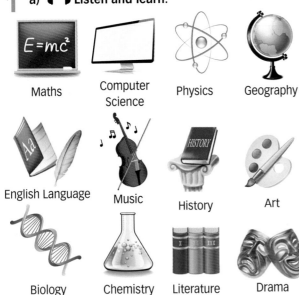

Maths

Computer Science

Physics

Geography

English Language

Music

History

Art

Biology

Chemistry

Literature

Drama

b) **Which subjects are/aren't you good at? What about your best friend? Tell your partner.**

I'm good at Maths. I'm not very good at History. My best friend is good at Physics. She isn't very good at Music. etc

Listening

2 a) **Look at the questions and answers. What is the dialogue about?**

1 Where is Elsa from?

  A Sweden   **B** Mexico   **C** Spain

2 How old is Carlos?

  A 21   **B** 20   **C** 18

3 What year is Elsa in?

  A 2   **B** 3   **C** 1

4 What is Diego's favourite subject?

  A English   **B** Geography   **C** Art

5 What is Carlos's favourite subject?

  A Chemistry   **B** Biology   **C** English

b) 🎧 **Listen and choose the correct answers.**

Everyday English
Greetings, Introductions & Personal questions

3 a) **Complete the dialogue.**

Ann:	Nice party!
Steve:	Yes, it's great.
Ann:	I'm Ann, by the way. **1)** .... is your name?
Steve:	I'm Steve, Steve Blair. Nice to meet you.
Ann:	Nice to meet you, too. **2)** .... are you from?
Steve:	I'm from Glasgow, Scotland.
Ann:	Oh, are you a student there?
Steve:	I'm a doctor. **3)** .... about you?
Ann:	I'm from Birmingham and I'm a student. I study Biology.
Steve:	Really? Biology is my favourite. **4)** .... old are you?
Ann:	I'm twenty-one. And you?
Steve:	Well, I'm thirty.

b) 🎧 **Listen and check.**

4 👥 **Act out a similar dialogue. Use phrases from the Language box.**

Greet people	Respond
• Hi!/Hello! How are you? • How's everything?	• Fine. • Great. • So-so. • Not bad. • I'm OK.
• Bye! • See you!	• See you!
Introduce yourself/others	**Respond**
• Hi! I'm ... . • Hello! My name's ... . This is	• Nice to meet you! • Oh, hi! I'm ... . • Pleased to meet you.
Personal questions	
• What's your name? • How old are you? • Where are you from? • What's your job?	

Intonation in *wh*-questions

5 **Read the theory.**
🎧 **Listen and repeat.**

> Intonation goes down at the end of ***wh-*** questions.
> *What's your name?* ↘

1 Where are you from?   **3** When is your birthday?

2 What's his name?   **4** What about you?

Reading & Writing

6 Read the texts. Copy and complete the table for each person in your notebook.

Michael Stephenson

About me:

My name's Michael. I'm 18 years old and I'm a college student from Los Angeles in the USA. My favourite subjects are Maths and Physics. I can swim and run very fast but I can't play the guitar. My favourite singer is Eminem.

Mumba Akua

About me:

I'm Mumba and I'm from Nairobi in Kenya. I'm 22 years old and I'm a college student. I'm crazy about Drama and Literature. My favourite writers are Oscar Wilde and F. Scott Fitzgerald. I can write really good stories and cook very well. I'm crazy about Sia. She's a great singer.

Name	
Age	
Where from	
Favourite subjects	
Abilities	
Favourite singer	

Writing Tip

Capital letters

In English we use capital letters to start a sentence. (*He's from Italy.*) We also use capital letters with:

- names (*Paul Smith*).
- school subjects (*Art*).
- countries (*Mexico*).
- nationalities (*Mexican*).
- days of the week (*Monday*).
- months (*June*).
- the personal pronoun *I*.

7 Read the *Writing Tip* box. Rewrite the sentences. Use capital letters.

1 i am from france. ....
2 you are interested in maths. ....
3 jenny can dance very well. ....
4 they are british. ....
5 my favourite sportsman is michael phelps. he's american.
....

Writing Tip

Linking ideas

- We use *and* to link similar ideas.
  I'm 25 years old and I'm from Vietnam.
- We use *but* to link opposing ideas.
  I can cook very well but I can't dance well.

8 Read the *Writing Tip* box. Use *and* or *but* to join the sentences.

1 Dan is 16 years old. He is good at Maths.
....
....

2 Mary can draw. She can't sing.
....
....

3 I am good at Music. I can play the piano very well.
....
....

4 I am interested in Drama. I can sing well.
....
....

5 Jenny can swim really fast. She can't cook very well.
....
....

Writing (an 'About me' profile)

9 Copy the table in Ex. 6 into your notebook and complete it with information about yourself.

10 You want to create your social media profile. Use your notes in Ex. 9 to write the 'About me' text for it (50-60 words).

VALUES

Unity

All for one and one for all.
Alexandre Dumas

1 Culture

▶ **VIDEO**

Countries of the English-speaking world

Over 840 million people speak English as a first or second language. It is an official language in 67 countries. And in these six countries most people are native speakers of English.

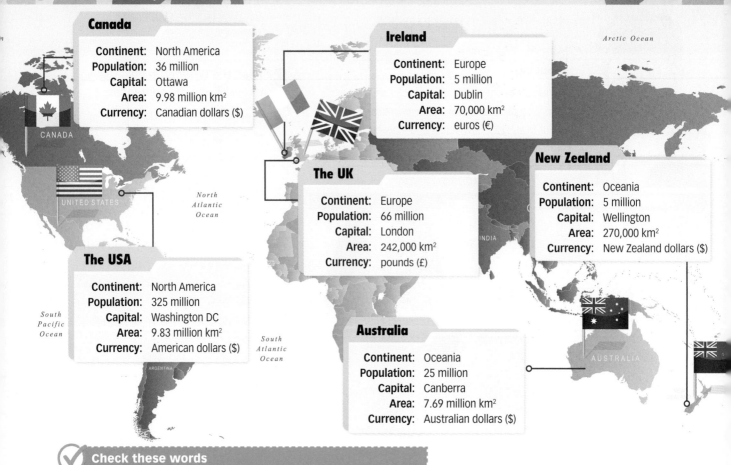

Canada
Continent:	North America
Population:	36 million
Capital:	Ottawa
Area:	9.98 million km²
Currency:	Canadian dollars ($)

Ireland
Continent:	Europe
Population:	5 million
Capital:	Dublin
Area:	70,000 km²
Currency:	euros (€)

The UK
Continent:	Europe
Population:	66 million
Capital:	London
Area:	242,000 km²
Currency:	pounds (£)

New Zealand
Continent:	Oceania
Population:	5 million
Capital:	Wellington
Area:	270,000 km²
Currency:	New Zealand dollars ($)

The USA
Continent:	North America
Population:	325 million
Capital:	Washington DC
Area:	9.83 million km²
Currency:	American dollars ($)

Australia
Continent:	Oceania
Population:	25 million
Capital:	Canberra
Area:	7.69 million km²
Currency:	Australian dollars ($)

✓ **Check these words**

official language, native speaker, continent, population, capital, currency

Listening & Reading

1 Look at the map and the fact files. What is the official language in these countries?
🎧 Listen and read the text to find out.

2 Read again and correct the sentences.

1 Australia and New Zealand are in North America.
2 Wellington is in Australia.
3 Ireland's currency is pounds.
4 Canada and the UK are nearly the same size.
5 The population of New Zealand is the same as the population of the UK.

Speaking & Writing

3 Use the colour guide 🎨 and say what colours are on each country's flag.

The UK's flag is red, white and blue.

4 Write a similar fact file about your country.

Vocabulary

1 **Write the numbers.**

1	5	....	**6**	3	....
2	15	....	**7**	38	....
3	12	....	**8**	105	....
4	20	....	**9**	16	....
5	73	....	**10**	82	....

(10 x 1 = 10)

2 **Write the nationalities.**

1 the UK – ....   **4** Turkey – ....

2 Japan – ....   **5** Spain – ....

3 Canada – ....

(5 x 2 = 10)

3 **Write each person's job.**

1 Terry can take good snapshots. ....

2 Anna can write interesting stories. ....

3 Jacob can design outfits. ....

4 Samantha can draw beautiful pictures. ....

5 Andrew can sing well. ....

(5 x 2 = 10)

Grammar

4 **Fill in the correct form of the verb** *to be*.

1 A: .... you a teacher?

B: No, I .... I .... a doctor.

2 A: .... Mark from the USA?

B: Yes, he .... He .... American.

3 A: .... Steve and Luke pilots?

B: No, they .... They .... actors.

4 A: .... you from Italy?

B: Yes, we .... We .... from Milan.

5 A: .... Julia from Germany?

B: No, she .... She .... from Russia.

(5 x 4 = 20)

5 **Fill in:** *a* or *an*.

I'm William and my best friend is Ben. He's **1)** ....
student at college and I'm **2)** .... actor. My
sister's **3)** .... artist. Ben's dream is to become
4) .... vet. It's **5)** .... amazing job.

(5 x 2 = 10)

6 **Use** *can* **or** *can't* **to fill in the gaps.**

1 "................... you cook?" "Yes, ..."

2 "................... we run fast?" "No, ..."

3 "................... Alison swim?" "Yes, ..."

4 "................... they dance?" "Yes, ..."

5 "................... he type fast?" "No, ..."

(5 x 2 = 10)

7 **Complete the gaps with the correct form of the verb** *to be* **or the verb** *can*.

I **1)** .... Kevin and this **2)** .... my friend Alex.
We **3)** .... best friends. Alex and I **4)** .... both
seventeen years old. My favourite subject **5)** ....
Music. I **6)** .... play the guitar, but I **7)** ....
sing very well. Alex **8)** .... really good at Art. He
9) .... draw amazing pictures. He **10)** ....
also take really good snapshots with his camera.

(10 x 2 = 20)

Everyday English

8 **Match the sentences.**

1 ☐ What's your name?   **A** I'm twenty.

2 ☐ How old are you?   **B** Not bad.

3 ☐ Hello! My name's   **C** She is from Mexico.
    Steve.   **D** I'm Brenda.

4 ☐ How are you?   **E** Nice to meet you!

5 ☐ Where is she from?

(5 x 2 = 10)

Total 100

Competences

GOOD ✓

VERY GOOD ✓ ✓

EXCELLENT ✓ ✓ ✓

Lexical Competence

Talk about

- cardinal numbers
- countries & nationalities
- jobs
- abilities
- colours

Reading Competence

- read for specific information (identify reference in a text; complete a table)

Listening Competence

- identify key information (multiple choice)

Speaking Competence

- greet & introduce myself/others
- give personal information

Writing Competence

- write a short text about my friend
- write an 'About me' page

Vocabulary: Family members, People's appearance, Character adjectives
Grammar: the verb *have got*, object/possessive pronouns, possessive adjectives, possessive case, *who's/whose*, plurals
Everyday English: Identifying & Describing people
Writing: A blog entry about a famous person

2 Families

Reading

1 **Look at the family tree. Who are these characters? Who's got a pet spider?**
Listen and read to find out.

VIDEO

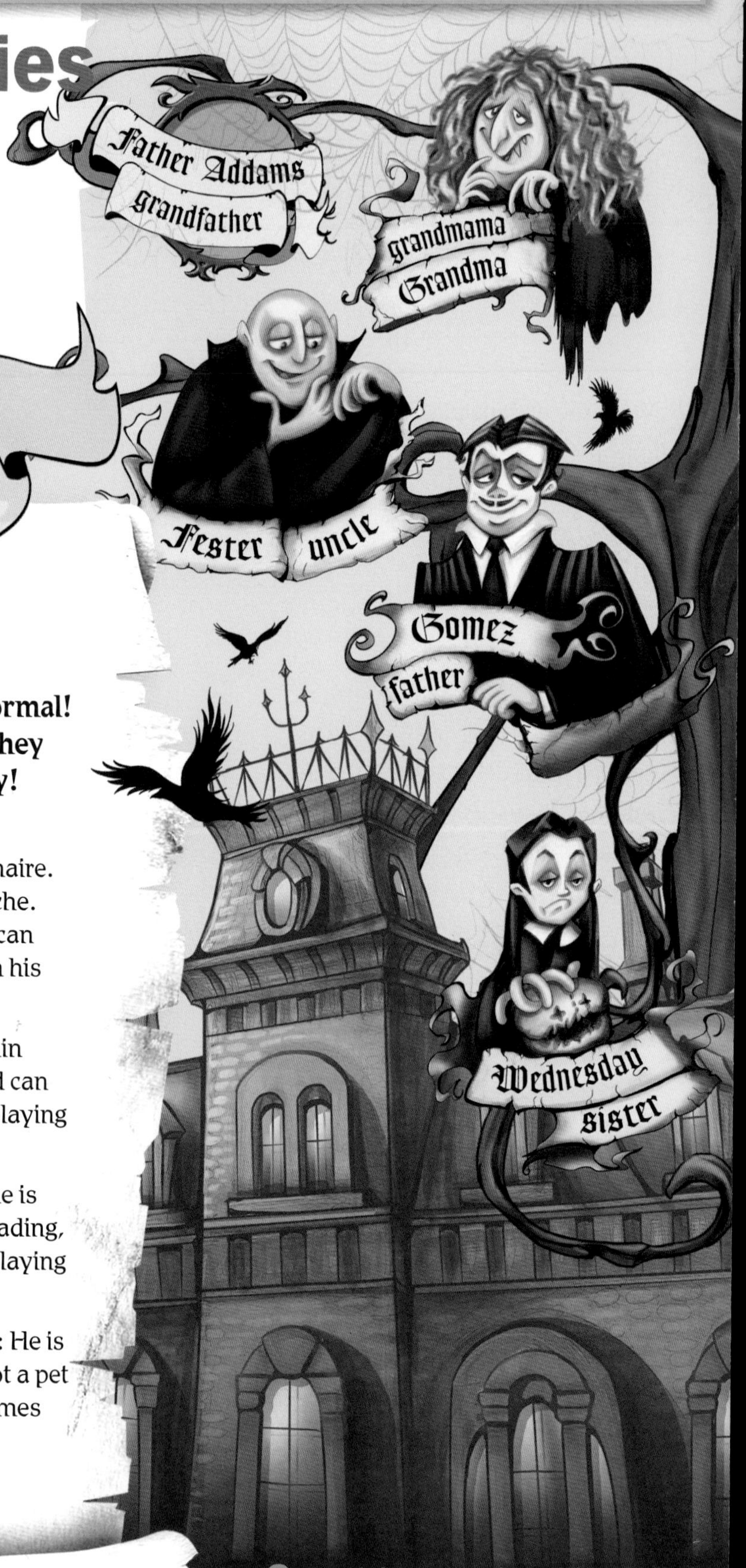

Father Addams
grandfather
grandmama
Grandma
Fester
uncle
Gomez
father
Wednesday
sister

A family like no other!

Imagine a family where nothing is normal! They are The Addams Family and they can make you laugh until you cry!

Gomez Addams (*husband*): He is a billionaire. He has got short black hair and a moustache. He can dance the tango with his wife and can juggle. His favourite hobby is playing with his toy trains.

Morticia Addams (*wife*): She is tall and thin with very long black hair. She is clever and can speak French. Her favourite hobbies are playing music and gardening.

Wednesday Addams (*their daughter*): She is very serious. Her favourite hobbies are reading, looking after her pet spider, Homer, and playing with her brother.

Pugsley Addams (*Wednesday's brother*): He is short, plump and very naughty. He has got a pet octopus; his name is Aristotle. Playing games with his sister is his favourite hobby.

Check these words

laugh, cry, billionaire, moustache, juggle, gardening, look after, naughty, octopus

2 **Read the text again and answer the questions.**

1. What is Gomez's favourite hobby?
2. What can Morticia do?
3. What is Wednesday like?
4. Who's got a pet octopus?

Vocabulary
Family members

3 Look at the family tree. Choose the correct word.

1 Fester is Gomez's **brother/father**.
2 Morticia is Ophelia's **daughter/sister**.
3 Wednesday is Grandmama's **aunt/granddaughter**.
4 Pubert is Ophelia's **son/nephew**.
5 Pugsley is Morticia's **cousin/son**.
6 Gomez is Morticia's **husband/father**.
7 Pugsley is Pubert's **brother/uncle**.
8 Father Frump and Grandma Frump are Wednesday's **parents/grandparents**.

4 Say a sentence about a person in the family tree. Your partner says who the person is.

A: *It's Father Frump's wife.*
B: *Grandma Frump.*

People's appearance

5 Look at the Addams' family tree. Who's:

1 **tall** and **slim** with **long straight black** hair?
2 **old** and **short** with **fair** hair?
3 **well-built** with **short** straight black hair and a moustache?
4 **young** and **plump** with **short** fair hair?
5 **middle-aged**, plump and **bald**?

6 Label the different parts of the face, then point to them on your face and name them.

- hair - mouth - nose - eye - cheek
- lips - teeth - chin - ear

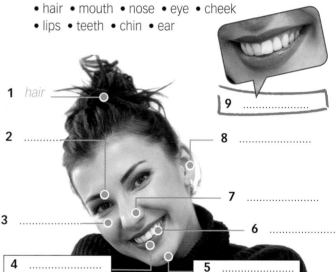

1 *hair*
2 ....
3 ....
4 ....
5 ....
6 ....
7 ....
8 ....
9 ....

Speaking & Writing

7 Use the words *small*, *short*, *fair*, *thin*, *curly*, *plump* to write the opposite phrases. Find photos of family/friends on your smartphone and show them to the class.

1 tall boy ≠ *short boy*
2 slim girl ≠ ....
3 long hair ≠ ....
4 straight hair ≠ ....
5 dark hair ≠ ....
6 full lips ≠ ....
7 big nose ≠ ....
8 big eyes ≠ ....

Speaking & Writing

8 Choose a person in the Addams family and ask and answer questions, as in the example.

A: *What does **Morticia** look like?*
B: ***She's tall** and **slim**. **She's got long straight black** hair.*

9 **ICT** Find pictures of another famous TV/film family. Label them. Present the family to the class.

13

Grammar in Use

Mary: *This photo is cool, but who are they?*
Beth: *They're my friends, Danny and his sister Jane.*
Mary: *Jane! Really?*
Beth: *Yes, she's got long dark hair now.*
Mary: *So, who's the girl with the curly hair?*
Beth: *That's Danny's cousin, Lynn. She's a vet. The new place on Cook Street is hers.*
Mary: *Really? Have you got her phone number? My dog's got a bad tooth.*
Beth: *No, sorry, I haven't. But we can ask Jane. She's got it.*

1 **Read the table. Find examples in the dialogue.**

The verb *have got*

Affirmative	
Long form	**Short form**
I/You have got … He/She/It has got … We/You/They have got …	I've/You've got … He's/She's/It's got … We've/You've/They've got …
Negative	
Long form	**Short form**
I/You have not got … He/She/It has not got … We/You/They have not got …	I/You haven't got … He/She/It hasn't got … We/You/They haven't got …
Interrogative	**Short answers**
Have I/you got …?	Yes, I/you have. / No, I/you haven't.
Has he/she/it got …?	Yes, he/she/it has. / No, he/she/it hasn't.
Have we/you/they got …?	Yes, we/you/they have. / No, we/you/they haven't.

2 **a) Look at the pictures and complete the sentences with:** *have got, has got, haven't got, hasn't got.*

1 John .... black hair. He .... fair hair.
2 Mary .... straight hair. She .... curly hair.
3 Ben and Andrea .... blonde hair. They .... brown hair.
4 Jessica .... long wavy hair. She .... short straight hair.
5 Charlotte and Mary .... short hair. They .... long hair.
6 Ben .... a beard and a moustache.
7 Andrea .... straight hair. She .... curly hair.
8 Daniel .... brown eyes, but Ben .... blue eyes.
9 Jessica .... fair hair. She .... dark hair.
10 Andrea and Charlotte .... long hair, but Jessica .... short hair.

b) **Form questions and then answer them, as in the example.**

1 Charlotte/fair hair?
2 Ben/a moustache?
3 Mary/brown eyes?
4 John/short hair?
5 Charlotte/blue eyes?
6 John/a beard?
7 Daniel/fair hair?
8 Jessica/red hair?
9 Andrea/straight hair?
10 Jessica/wavy hair?

1 A: Has Charlotte got fair hair?
B: No, she hasn't. She's got red hair.

14

3 SPEAKING Choose one person from Ex. 2. Your partner asks questions to find out who this person is.

A: Is it a woman?
B: Yes, it is.

A: Has she got brown hair?
B: Yes, she has.

4 Read the table. Find examples in the dialogue on p. 14.

Object pronouns – Possessive adjectives/pronouns

Object Pronouns	me	you	him	her	it	us	you	them
after the verb as objects: *Look at **him**. He's my friend.*								
Possessive Adjectives	my	your	his	her	its	our	your	their
before nouns to show possession: *This is **his** dog.*								
Possessive pronouns	mine	yours	his	hers	—	ours	yours	theirs
at the end of a sentence: *It's **his**.*								

5 Choose the correct item.

✉ Meet the Swansons!

Hello readers! **1) My/I** name is Mark and **2) I/me** am 23 years old. I've got short brown hair and **3) my/me** eyes are blue. In this photo, I am with **4) my/me** brother Tom and **5) us/our** sister Ann. **6) We/Us** are at the beach. Look at **7) we/us**. Tom is 25 years old. **8) Him/He**'s very tall and well-built. **9) Our/Us** sister Ann is 20 years old.**10) She/Her** is a bit short and **11) she/her** hair is brown. She's very funny. Tell **12) us/our** about your families.

6 Read the theory. Find an example in the dialogue on p. 14.

Possessive case ('/'s)

We use:
- **'s** with **singular** and **irregular plural nouns**. *the boy**'s** brother, the men**'s** father*
- **'** with **plural nouns**. *the girls**'** mother*
- **of** to talk about **things that belong to other things**. *the door **of** the car*

COMPARE: *Jo and Sue's brothers* (same brothers)
BUT: *Jo's and Sue's brothers* (different brothers)
- We use **who** to ask about **people**. *Who is Tony?*
- We use **whose** to ask about **possession** or **relation**. *Whose cat is this? Whose brother is Tony?*

7 Choose the correct item.

1 **Who's/Whose** brother is Mike? He's **Kelly's/Kellys'** brother.
2 **Who/Whose** is Bill? He is the **boy's/boys** cousin.
3 **Who/Whose** is Mark? He's **Sam's and Mary's/Sam and Mary's** brother.
4 Where are **John's and Ann's/John and Ann's** rooms?
5 These are the **girls'/girl's** glasses. They are their glasses.

8 Read the theory. Find an example in the dialogue on p. 14.

Plurals

- nouns + **-s**: *one friend – two friends*
- **-s**, **-ss**, **-sh**, **-ch**, **-x**, **-o** + **-es**: *bus – buses, glass – glasses, brush – brushes, match – matches, box – boxes, tomato – tomatoes*
- **-f**, **-fe** → **-ves**: *leaf – leaves, knife – knives*
- consonant **-y** → **-ies**: *family – families* **BUT:** *boy – boys*
- **Irregular plurals:** *man – **men**, woman – **women**, child – **children**, foot – **feet**, tooth – **teeth**, ox – **oxen**, deer – **deer**, fish – **fish**, sheep – **sheep***

9 Use the plural form of the nouns in the brackets to complete the gaps.

Hi, I'm Louise. Meet my family.
1 I've got two .... **(brother)**, Peter and Ralph.
2 Their .... **(personality)** are very different from each other.
3 Peter's favourite .... **(hobby)** are reading and listening to music.
4 Ralph's got three .... **(goldfish)**.
5 My dad is a teacher at two .... **(university)**.
6 My mum is an artist. She can create beautiful .... **(painting)** with her .... **(brush)**.
7 I've got four of them in my room. My favourite is the one with brown .... **(leaf)**.

10 SPEAKING Show photos of your friends on your smartphone. Your partner asks questions about them. Use the dialogue on p. 14 as a model.

15

Skills in Action

Vocabulary
Character adjectives

1 **a)** 🎧 **Listen and learn.**

> **Study Skills**
>
> **Opposites**
> Learn words with their opposites. This helps you remember them.

outgoing ≠ shy   clever ≠ silly

hard-working ≠ lazy   quiet ≠ noisy

funny ≠ serious   kind ≠ impolite

b) Which adjectives best describe you?

I'm funny and kind. I can be noisy at times.

Listening

> **Study Skills**
>
> **Multiple matching**
> Read the rubric and the lists of words. Try to guess the content of the recording. While you listen, try not to get distracted as all options will be mentioned.

2 **a)** 🎧 **Listen to Tom talking to a friend. Match the people to their relationship with Tom.**

People		Relation	
0	[B] Alex	**A**	cousin
1	☐ Margaret	**B**	brother
2	☐ Martha	**C**	aunt
3	☐ David	**D**	mum
4	☐ Claire	**E**	dad
5	☐ Michelle	**F**	grandma
		G	uncle
		H	sister

b) 🎧 **Listen again. What is each person like?**

Everyday English
Identifying & Describing people

3 🎧 **Use the sentences A-D to complete the dialogue. One sentence is extra. Listen and check. Find Mr Jones in the picture.**

A Who is Mr Jones?   **C** How old is he?
B What's his name?   **D** What's he like?

Ann:	1) ....
Jane:	He's the one with the short fair hair, beard and moustache.
Ann:	2) ....
Jane:	I think he's 35.
Ann:	3) ....
Jane:	Well, he's really quiet and he's very hard-working.
Ann:	OK. Let's go into the meeting.

4 👥 **You are about to go into a meeting. Act out a dialogue similar to the one in Ex. 3. Use phrases from the language box.**

Asking about people	Responding
• What is he/she like?	• He/She's clever.
• How old is he/she?	• He/She's 25.
• Who's he/she?	• He/She's the new manager etc.
• What's his/her name?	• Mr Smith/Ms Brown etc.

Pronunciation /iː/ /ɪ/

5 🎧 **Listen and tick (✓). Listen again and repeat.**

	/iː/	/ɪ/		/iː/	/ɪ/		/iː/	/ɪ/
six			three			teacher		
read			slim			singer		

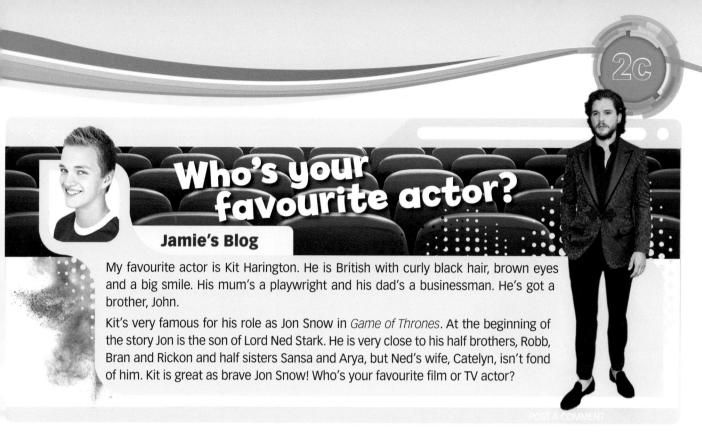

Who's your favourite actor?

Jamie's Blog

My favourite actor is Kit Harington. He is British with curly black hair, brown eyes and a big smile. His mum's a playwright and his dad's a businessman. He's got a brother, John.

Kit's very famous for his role as Jon Snow in *Game of Thrones*. At the beginning of the story Jon is the son of Lord Ned Stark. He is very close to his half brothers, Robb, Bran and Rickon and half sisters Sansa and Arya, but Ned's wife, Catelyn, isn't fond of him. Kit is great as brave Jon Snow! Who's your favourite film or TV actor?

POST A COMMENT

Reading & Writing

6 Look at the text. What is it about? Read and check.

7 Read again and answer the questions.

1 Where is Kit Harington from?

....

2 What is his mum's job?

....

3 Which TV series is he in?

....

4 Who's Jon Snow's dad?

....

5 What is Jon Snow like?

....

✎ Writing Tip

Punctuation

We use a(n) ...

- (.) **full stop** after affirmative & negative sentences.
- (?) **question mark** after interrogative sentences.
- (,) **comma** to separate a list of items.
- (!) **exclamation mark** to express strong feelings.

8 Punctuate the following sentences.

1 His real name is Christopher

2 His hair isn't black

3 Who's your favourite actor

4 He's an actor a writer and a poet

5 He is amazing

9 **ICT** Collect information about your favourite actor/actress. Answer the questions.

1 Who's your favourite actor/actress?

....

2 Where's he/she from?

....

3 Has he/she got any brothers/sisters/sons/daughters?

....

4 Which film/TV series is he/she in?

....

5 What is he/she like in his/her role?

....

Writing

(A blog entry about a famous person)

10 Use your answers from Ex. 9 to write a blog entry about your favourite actor/actress similar to the one in Ex. 6 (50-80 words). Follow the plan.

Plan

Para 1: name of favourite actor/actress, nationality, appearance and family members.

Para 2: name in film/TV series, family, character

VALUES

Family

Family is not an important thing. It's everything.

Michael J. Fox

▶ VIDEO

Celebrity Siblings

It's easy to be famous with a brother or sister by your side!

The Franco brothers

There's not one, not two, but THREE Franco brothers! They are the sons of a businessman and a writer from California. They are all very clever and talented. James and Dave are both actors. James is outgoing but Dave is quite shy. Tom is an actor too, but he is also an artist. He's very funny.

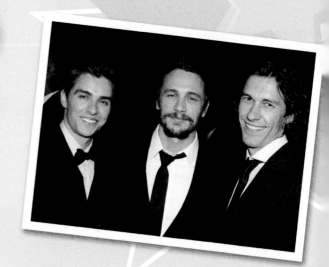

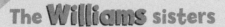

The Williams sisters

These two sisters are great tennis players. They are both very hard-working. Venus is Serena's big sister. Their dad Richard, their ex-coach, and their mum Oracene Price, are very proud of their daughters. The sisters have got homes in Florida very near one another. Because of their love of fashion, they have both got clothing companies.

Listening & Reading

1 Look at the photos. Who are these people? Whose dad is a businessman?

🎧 Listen and read to find out.

2 Read the text again and replace the words in bold with words from the text.

1 Venus and Serena can play **it**.
2 Venus is **her** big sister.
3 Venus' and Serena's houses are **there**.
4 The Franco brothers are from **there**.
5 **He** is shy.
6 **He** is an artist.

✓ **Check these words**

sibling, famous, ex-coach, proud, fashion, company, talented

Speaking & Writing

3 👥 Ask and answer questions about the siblings.

• Who's ...? • What does ... look like?
• What is ... like?

4 **ICT** Work in groups. Write short descriptions about famous siblings in your country or other countries. Write about: *names*, *jobs*, *character*. Present them to the class.

Vocabulary

1 **Complete the sentences.**

```
        Jonathan ──┬── Valeria
                   │
        ┌──────────┴──────┐
Victoria ──┬── Ben    Helen ──┬── David
     ┌─────┼─────┐      ┌──────┼──────┐
   Peter Sarah Ryan   Mary  Jason  Daisy
```

1 Valeria is Helen's ....
2 Ben is Ryan's ....
3 Jason is Sarah's ....
4 Peter is Helen's ....
5 Victoria is Daisy's ....

(5 x 2 = 10)

2 **Match to form collocations.**

1 ☐ old   A lips
2 ☐ straight   B woman
3 ☐ full   C nose
4 ☐ big   D hair

(4 x 2 = 8)

3 **Write the opposites.**

1 long hair ≠ ....   4 noisy boy ≠ ....
2 tall boy ≠ ....   5 straight hair ≠ ....
3 thin girl ≠ ....   6 funny boy ≠ ....

(6 x 2 = 12)

Grammar

4 **Complete with:** *has, hasn't, have, haven't.*

1 .... you got a brother? No, I ....
2 .... Gavin got black hair? Yes, he ....
3 .... your parents got fair hair? No, they ....
4 .... Andy and Mary got two children?
   Yes, they ....
5 .... your mum got curly hair? No, she ....

(5 x 2 = 10)

5 **Choose the correct item.**

1 Look at **us/we**. **Our/We**'ve got beards.
2 **My/Me** brother is twenty. Look at **him/his**!
3 This isn't **your/yours** ball. It's **me/mine**.
4 This is **them/their** dog. It's **them/theirs**.

(4 x 2 = 8)

6 **Write the plurals.**

1 hobby – ....   4 child – ....
2 brother – ....   5 foot – ....
3 man – ....   6 fish – ....

(6 x 2 = 12)

7 **Choose the correct item.**

1 **Whose/Who's** sister is this?
   This is **Vicky's/Vickys'** sister.
2 **Whose/Who's** that over there?
   She is **Tom's and Anna's/Tom and Anna's** sister.
3 **Whose/Who's** are all these boxes?
   They are the **girl's/girls** boxes.
4 **Whose/Who** is he over there?
   He's **George's/Georges'** brother.
5 **Whose/Who** dad is Sean?
   He is **Mary and Ann's/Mary's and Ann's** dad.

(5 x 4 = 20)

Everyday English

8 **Match the exchanges.**

1 ☐ Who's he?   A He's 17.
2 ☐ What's his name?   B He's quiet.
3 ☐ How old is he?   C John.
4 ☐ What does he look   D He's tall and well-built.
     like?   E He's my cousin.
5 ☐ What's he like?

(5 x 4 = 20)
Total 100

Competences

GOOD ✓

VERY GOOD ✓ ✓

EXCELLENT ✓ ✓ ✓

Lexical Competence
Talk about
• family members
• people's appearance
• character adjectives

Reading Competence
• read for specific information (identify information in a text; answer questions)

Listening Competence
• multiple matching (identify relationships)

Speaking Competence
• identify and describe people

Writing Competence
• write short texts about a famous family and famous siblings
• write a blog entry about my favourite famous person

Vocabulary:	Rooms, Furniture, Appliances, Ordinal numbers, Types of houses
Grammar:	*there is/are*, *a/an/some/any*, *this/these*, *that/those*, prepositions of place
Everyday English:	Renting a flat
Writing:	An email describing your new flat

Home sweet home!

Vocabulary

Furniture & Appliances

1 Look at the picture of the house. Which rooms are:

- on the ground floor (downstairs)?
- on the first floor (upstairs)?
- in the attic?
- outside the house?

The kitchen is on the ground floor downstairs.

2 Put the furniture/appliances in each room.

🎧 Listen and check.

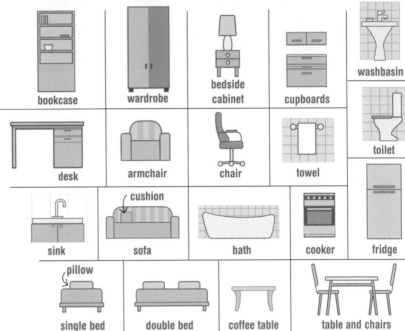

bookcase · wardrobe · bedside cabinet · cupboards · washbasin · desk · armchair · chair · towel · toilet · sink · cushion · sofa · bath · cooker · fridge · pillow · single bed · double bed · coffee table · table and chairs

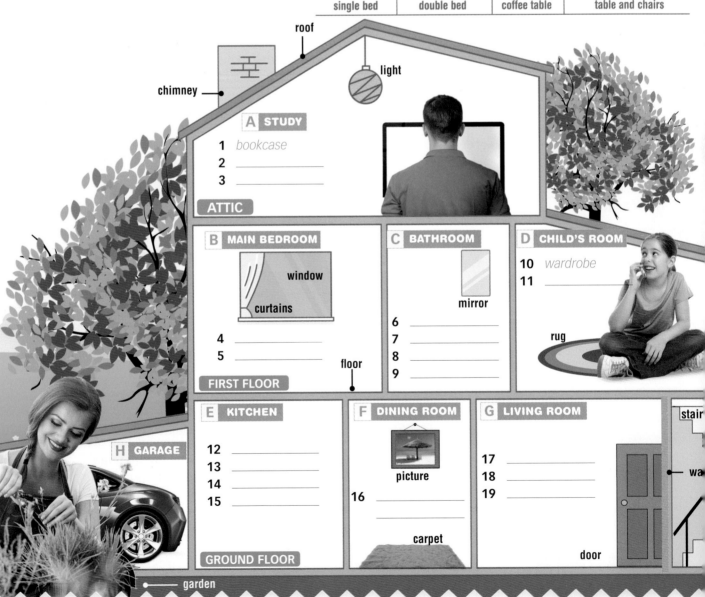

| Home | About Us | Special Offers | Destinations | Booking | FAQ | ▶ VIDEO |

Life underground

Can people today live under the ground? In an area in Spain, far away from the **big** cities, there is a small city called Guadix. In one neighbourhood, all you can see are white chimneys, red roofs and small wooden doors. This is because the houses there are not on the hills, they are under them!

These **unique** cave houses are very old; some of them are over 1,000 years old. But they all have **modern** furniture and appliances.

In a typical cave house there is a **cosy** kitchen with a **wonderful** view of a **beautiful** garden. There is also a huge bathroom, a **large** bedroom and a **spacious** living room.

These **pretty** homes are good for the environment. Since they're underground, they can save electricity as they are cool in the summer and warm in the winter.

For people in Guadix, this neighbourhood is very special. It's a world away from the noisy life of the city.

✓ **Check these words**

ground, neighbourhood, wooden, hill, environment, save, cool, warm

Easy Travel

Terms | Contacts

Reading

3 Look at the pictures. What is special about these houses?

🎧 Listen and read to find out.

4 Read the text again and decide if the sentences are *T* (True) or *F* (False).

1 There are cave houses in all cities in Spain. ....
2 The cave houses have got red chimneys. ....
3 They have got wooden doors. ....
4 There are some new cave houses in Guadix. ....
5 A typical cave house has got four rooms. ....

5 Look at the adjectives in bold in the text and fill in the nouns.

1 big *cities*
2 unique ....
3 modern ....
4 cosy ....
5 wonderful ....

6 beautiful ....
7 huge ....
8 large ....
9 spacious ....
10 pretty ....

6 Write the adjectives in Ex. 5 that have a similar meaning to the adjectives in bold.

1 **lovely** = *wonderful*, b _ _ _ _ _ _ _ _ , p_ _ _ _ _
2 **big** = h _ _ _ , l _ _ _ _ , s_ _ _ _ _ _ _

Speaking & Writing

7 (THINK) How different is your house from a typical cave house? Write a few sentences. Read them to the class.

Study Skills

Grouping words

Grouping words under headings helps you to remember new vocabulary.

8 👥 Group the words in Exs 1 and 2 under the headings: *rooms – furniture – appliances – other/ decoration*.

9 (THINK) Which is your favourite room in your house? Why? Describe it.

21

Grammar in Use

Homes   For rent   For sale

Spacious house in Edgbaston, Birmingham

This unique house has got four bedrooms, one kitchen, two bathrooms, one living room and a study. Outside there is a garage, a small garden in front of the house and a large one behind it. The kitchen, the living room and the study are on the ground floor. Upstairs there are the bedrooms and the bathrooms. This is a great home for all the family.

Make it yours today!
Contact Mr Bernard on 01218...

1 a) **Read the theory. Find examples in the advert.**

there is/there are – a/an – some/any

Singular		Plural
There **is a/an** ...	**Affirmative**	There **are some** ...
There **isn't a/an** ...	**Negative**	There **aren't any** ...
Is there **a/an** ...?	**Interrogative**	**Are** there **any** ...?
Yes, there **is**. **No**, there **isn't**.	**Short Answers**	**Yes**, there **are**./ **No**, there **aren't**.

- We use **there is** in the singular.
  There is a bed in the bedroom.
- We use **there are** in the plural.
  There are two beds in the bedroom.
- We use **some** in the plural in the affirmative.
  There are some chairs in the kitchen.
- We use **any** in the plural in the negative and the interrogative. *There aren't any chairs in the kitchen. Are there any chairs in the kitchen?*

b) **Complete the sentences with** there is/isn't, there are/aren't, is/are there.

1 A: .... any chairs in the kitchen?
   B: No, ...
2 A: .... a desk in the bedroom?
   B: Yes, ...
3 A: .... a fireplace in the living room?
   B: No, ...
4 A: .... any cushions on the sofa?
   B: Yes, ...

2 **Complete the sentences with** some/any, a/an.

1 There is .... table in our kitchen.
2 There are .... pillows on the bed.
3 Are there .... flowers in the vase?
4 Is there .... bookcase in your living room?
5 There is .... armchair in our study.
6 There aren't .... cars in the garage.
7 There are .... books on the desk.
8 Is there .... fireplace in your house?
9 There is .... painting on the wall.
10 There is .... attic in the house.

3 a) **What things can you see in the picture? Put a tick (✓) or a cross (✗) for each, then ask and answer questions, as in the example.**

1	dining table	✗	9	double bed	....
2	bedside cabinets	✓	10	single bed	....
3	cushions	....	11	light	....
4	pillows	....	12	desk	....
5	posters	....	13	rug	....
6	lamps	....	14	bookcase	....
7	sofa	....	15	curtains	....
8	armchair	....	16	fireplace	....

A: *Is there a dining table?*
B: *No, there isn't. Are there any bedside cabinets?*
A: *Yes, there are. etc.*

b) 👥 **Describe the picture. Make three mistakes. Your partner corrects you.**

4 **Read the theory.**

this/these – that/those

- We use **this/these** for things **near** us.
  This is my bed. These are my cushions. (near)
- We use **that/those** for things **far from** us.
  That is my desk. Those are my posters. (far)

22

5 Write sentences as in the example.

1 *This is a sofa and that is a coffee table.*

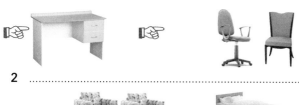

2 ....

3 ....

4 ....

5 ....

Ordinal numbers

6 🎧 Listen and learn. Which floor are the people's flats on?

nineteenth	19	20	twentieth
seventeenth	17	18	eighteenth
fifteenth	15	16	sixteenth
thirteenth	13	14	fourteenth
eleventh	11	12	twelfth
ninth	9	10	tenth
seventh	7	8	eighth
fifth	5	6	sixth
third	3	4	fourth
first	1	2	second
basement	-1	0	ground floor

Steve & Paul **9th**

Tony & Larry **8th**

Jane **1st**

y **3rd**

Sue & Ann **12th**

Prepositions of place

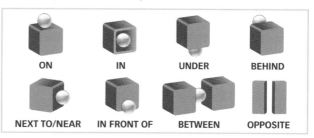

ON — IN — UNDER — BEHIND

NEXT TO/NEAR — IN FRONT OF — BETWEEN — OPPOSITE

7 Look at the sketches and the picture, then choose the correct preposition.

This is our living room. There are two sofas with some cushions **1) in/on** them. There is a vase **2) opposite/on** the coffee table with flowers **3) in/behind** it and a rug **4) behind/on** the floor **5) under/in front of** the coffee table. The coffee table is **6) between/opposite** the fireplace and the sofa. **7) Behind/Next to** the fireplace there is a TV. There is also a chair **8) behind/in front of** the TV and a huge window **9) opposite/next to** it. Our living room is very modern.

8 👥 Look at the picture. Use the words to ask and answer questions, as in the example.

- desk • bed
- ball • rug
- wardrobe
- pillow
- bedside cabinet
- window • chair
- lamp

A: *Where's the desk?* B: *It's next to the wardrobe.*

9 THINK 💬 Design your ideal house. How many floors has it got? What are the rooms like? What furniture is there? What colours are the walls? Present it to the class.

10 WRITING Write an advert for your house. Use the advert on p. 22 as a model.

23

Skills in Action

Vocabulary

Types of houses

1 🎧 Listen and learn. Which of these types of houses are there in your city/village?

UK HOUSES

block of flats

terraced

detached

semi-detached

Study Skills

Note taking (Predicting words)
Try to guess what is missing in each gap (e.g. a name, a noun, a number). This will help you do the task.

Listening

2 Look at gaps 1-5. Which ask for: *a number*? *a noun*? *an adjective*?

🎧 Listen to an estate agent and a flat owner and complete the gaps.

Large Flat Available for Rent

Address: [1] Greenbank Park

Rooms: a [2] living room, a kitchen, a small bathroom and two [3] bedrooms

Outside: a small garden and a double [4]

Cost: £800 per [5]

Read More

Everyday English

Renting a flat

3 a) Max wants to rent a flat and he is talking to an estate agent. Complete the dialogue with the phrases (A-E).

Estate Agent:	Hello. How can I help you?
Max:	Yes. **1)** ....
Estate Agent:	Okay, let me see. There is a very nice flat for rent very close to the city centre.
Max:	**2)** ....
Estate Agent:	It's 14 Oakfield Road.
Max:	Oh, OK. **3)** ....
Estate Agent:	It's a double bedroom flat. It has got a living room, dining room, kitchen and two bathrooms.
Max:	And which floor is it on?
Estate Agent:	It's on the second floor of a nice block of flats.
Max:	**4)** ....
Estate Agent:	It's £500 per month.
Max:	That's perfect. **5)** ....
Estate Agent:	Of course, I can take you there right now.
Max:	That's great.

A How many rooms has it got?

B How much is the rent?

C Can I see it?

D I'm interested in a flat near the city centre.

E What's the address?

b) 🎧 Listen and check.

4 👥 You want to rent the flat in Ex. 2. Act out a similar dialogue to the one in Ex. 3. Use phrases from the language box.

Asking information about a flat	Giving information about a flat
• How many rooms has it got? • Which floor is it on? • How much is the rent? • What's the address?	• It's got *(two bedrooms, one kitchen)*, etc. • It's on the *(second)* floor. • It's *(£500)* per month. • It's *(87 Ridgeway Street)*.

Pronunciation /ɑː/ /æ/

5 🎧 Listen and tick (✓). Listen again and repeat.

	/ɑː/	/æ/		/ɑː/	/æ/		/ɑː/	/æ/
attic			carpet			armchair		
garden			lamp			flat		

Reading & Writing

6 Look at the email. Who is it from? Who is it for? What is it about? Read through to find out.

From: Gina
To: Dad
Subject: My new home

Hi Dad,

1 Thanks for the beautiful paintings! I'm in my new flat, at last! It's on the seventh floor of a huge block of flats near the city centre and it's got a wonderful view of a park outside. It's got a large living room, a small bathroom, a modern kitchen and a bedroom.

2 My bedroom's wonderful. There's a double bed and a desk. The wardrobe's very small, but that's OK. There are some beautiful paintings on the walls now.

3 My new flat is very comfortable. Can't wait for you to come and see it. Drop me a line soon.

Bye for now!

Gina

Study Skills

Paragraphs
Always group your ideas into paragraphs. A new idea needs a new paragraph.

7 Read again. Which paragraph is: *a description of the flat*? *a description of Gina's room*?

Writing Tip

Informal language
When we write emails to people we know like our friends and family we use informal language. That is:
- everyday vocabulary. *(Thanks, at last)*
- everyday expressions and idioms. *(Drop me a line.)*
- short verb forms. *(I'm in my new flat.)*
- omission of pronouns. *(Can't wait* instead of *I can't wait)*

8 Find examples of informal language in the email in Ex. 6.

Writing (an email describing your new flat)

9 Read the task. Answer the questions.

You are in London starting college. This is part of an email from your Australian friend.

> What's life like in London? Is your flat OK? What is your bedroom like? Write back.

Write an email to your friend answering all the questions (80 words).

1 What are you going to write? ....
2 Who is it for? ....
3 What should you write about? ....
4 How many words should you write? ....

Study Skills

Brainstorming
Before you start writing, brainstorm for ideas. This helps you do the writing task.

10 **a)** Complete the spidergram in your notebook with information about your flat/house.

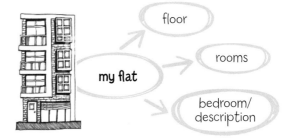

b) Use your notes in Ex. 10a to write your email. Follow the plan.

Plan

Hi + (friend's first name),
Para 1: opening remarks; describe your house (number of rooms, location, extra features)
Para 2: describe your bedroom (colour, objects in it)
Para 3: closing remarks
Bye for now!
(your first name)

3 Culture

The UK - Homes of the Monarchy ▶ VIDEO

The Royal Family of the UK are very powerful people. The Queen is the UK's head of state. Their homes are very impressive.

A

Windsor Castle is the weekend home of the British monarchy. It is in the county of Berkshire, England. It is a very old building. Actually, it is over 900 years old. It has got very high walls and a large tower in the middle of it with lots of rooms.

C

St James's Palace is one of the homes of the monarch of the UK and the Royal Court. The palace is a large building in London, next to St James's Park. It is over 400 years old and it has got tall red walls and a big gatehouse at the front. Inside, there are lots of rooms and offices.

B

Buckingham Palace is the official home of the monarchy of the UK in London. It is in the centre of London next to Hyde Park. It is a huge building with 775 rooms. There are 52 royal bedrooms, 188 staff bedrooms and 78 bathrooms in it.

People from all over the world can visit these homes and see the amazing paintings, spacious rooms and pretty gardens of the UK's monarchy. They are open for all.

✓ **Check these words**

powerful, head of state, county, gatehouse, office

Listening & Reading

1 Look at the pictures. Where is each building?
🎧 Listen and read to find out.

2 Read the texts again. Which building(s) A, B or C ...

has got offices?	1 ☐
are near a park?	2 ☐ ☐
has got high walls?	3 ☐
are in London?	4 ☐ ☐
has got red walls?	5 ☐

Speaking & Writing

3 ⟨THINK⟩ Which of the three buildings is the most impressive? Why?

4 ICT 👥 Think of the head of state in your country. Is there a special building for them to live in? Collect information under the headings: *location – age – size – rooms*. **Present it to the class.**

Vocabulary

1 Find the odd word out.

1 living room – study – attic – pillow
2 bath – washbasin – toilet – garden
3 garage – bed – bedside cabinet – wardrobe
4 terraced – detached – semi-detached – bathroom
5 window – cushion – chimney – wall
6 castle – block of flats – terraced – stairs
7 sofa – cooker – fridge – sink
8 table – chairs – window – sofa
9 chimney – roof – cooker – window

(9 x 2 = 18)

2 Fill in: *cushions, armchairs, rug, mirror, wardrobe, towels, pillows, curtains*.

1 In the bathroom there are some colourful .... and a .... on the wall.
2 In my bedroom there is a .... next to my bed and a .... on the floor.
3 There are two .... with some .... in the living room.
4 On my bed there are two large .... and yellow .... on the window.

(8 x 2 = 16)

Grammar

3 Use *is/isn't, are/aren't* and *some/any/a/an* to complete the description of this room.

1 In my bedroom there .... single bed but there .... wardrobe.
2 There .... pillow on the bed but there .... cushions.
3 There .... armchair but there .... chair.
4 There .... bookcase but there .... shelves on the walls.
5 There .... desk but there .... TV.
6 There .... pencils on the desk but there .... computer.

(12 x 2 = 24)

4 Fill in: *this/that, these/those*.

1 .... is a vase and .... are flowers.

2 .... are posters and .... is a painting.

3 .... are cushions and .... is an armchair.

(6 x 2 = 12)

5 Choose the correct item.

1 There is a large window **behind/on** the desk.
2 There is a rug **above/on** the floor.
3 The posters **in/on** the wall are really nice.
4 There is a bedside cabinet **next to/behind** the bed.
5 The armchair is **between/in front of** the fireplace.
6 The flowers **in/under** the vase are beautiful.
7 The wardrobe is **opposite/above** the bed.
8 The bed is **between/in front of** the two bedside cabinets.
9 The rug is **under/above** the table.
10 The painting **under/above** the fireplace is really old.

(10 x 1 = 10)

Everyday English

6 Match the two columns.

1 ☐ Which floor is your flat on?
2 ☐ How many rooms has it got?
3 ☐ How much is the rent?
4 ☐ What's the address?
5 ☐ How can I help you?

A It's £600 per month.
B On the sixth.
C It's got six.
D I'm interested in a flat.
E It's 64 Benson Street.

(5 x 4 = 20)

Total 100

Competences

GOOD ✓
VERY GOOD ✓ ✓
EXCELLENT ✓ ✓ ✓

Lexical Competence
Talk about:
• rooms, furniture & appliances
• ordinal numbers
• types of houses

Reading Competence
• read for specific information (T/F statements; multiple matching)
Listening Competence
• listen for detail (note taking)

Speaking Competence
• renting a flat
Writing Competence
• write an advert for my house
• write an email describing my new flat

Values: National pride

▶ VIDEO

India · Myanmar · Uruguay · Egypt · Nigeria · Fiji

Every country in the world has got a flag.

The different shapes and colours on a flag are symbols of the values the people from each country have. Flags are also national symbols.

Colours

Red is for life, courage and strength. You can see red on the flags of Egypt, Poland and Vietnam.

Blue is for water, sky, wisdom and honesty. You can see blue on the flags of Kazakhstan, Fiji and Thailand.

Green is for nature, peace and harmony. You can see green on the flags of Mexico, Brazil and Nigeria.

Symbols

The **Sun** is a symbol of energy. Countries like Uruguay, Namibia and Argentina have got it on their flags.

Stars are a symbol of power. Myanmar, Cuba and Chile have all got stars on their flags.

Stripes are a symbol of freedom. Many countries, like France, Poland and India, have got stripes on their flags.

---

1 Look at the flags. Why are the colours and symbols on them important?
🎧 Listen and read to find out.

2 Read again and complete the table in your notebook. Choose two flags and explain what the colours and symbols on them mean.

colours	meaning	symbols	meaning
red		the Sun	
blue		stars	
green		stripes	

3 ICT 💬 Collect information about the meaning of more colours and more symbols on flags. Prepare a poster. Tell the class.

4 THINK 💬 Imagine your team takes part in a sports competition. You need to create your own flag. Decide on: *colours, symbols, meanings*. Use the information in Ex. 2 to design your flag.

5 You are your team's representative. Present your team's flag to the audience. Explain its meaning. The class votes for the best idea.

Public Speaking Skills

Study Skills

Preparing your presentation: steps to follow

A Brainstorm for ideas. Collect information and create a spidergram with notes.

B Find appropriate visuals.

C Prepare your presentation. Use your notes to write your text.

D Practise your presentation in front of a mirror.

E Give your presentation. Speak clearly. Use short sentences. Look at the audience. Use appropriate body language and gestures. Smile. Don't cross your arms, put your hands in your pockets or look at your notes all the time.

1 a) Read the task.

Imagine you celebrate Flag Day at a local event. You are the school's representative. Present your country's flag to the audience.

b) 🎧 **Listen and read the model. Then copy and complete the spidergram in your notebook.**

Hello, I'm Lien Dao.

You can see it on public buildings during national celebrations in Vietnam. What is it? … That's right! It's the flag of Vietnam. I'm from Vietnam and one of the things I'm proud of is my country's flag.

Vietnam's flag is red and has got a yellow star on it. The red is for life and the yellow is for the people of Vietnam. The five points on the star are for the soldiers, traders, students, farmers and workers of Vietnam.

The flag is our country's national symbol and it has a special meaning for us — just like the flags of other countries have a special meaning to their people. Thank you for listening.

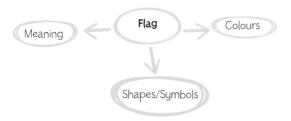

2 Read the theory. Which opening technique can you read in the model?

Opening techniques in public speaking

To start a presentation, we can:

- **Use humour/a riddle:** "I am red with a yellow star and I am a symbol of my country. What am I? … It's the flag of my country, Vietnam."
- **Address the audience directly:** "Can you guess the meaning of the colour on this flag?"
- **Ask a rhetorical question:** "Aren't we proud of our country's flag?"
- **Make a statement:** "One thing I'm proud of is my country's flag."

3 Copy the spidergram in Ex. 1b and complete it with information about the flag of your country. Use your notes and the model to prepare and give your presentation.

29

Busy days

Vocabulary: Daily routines, Days of the week, Telling the time, Free-time activities, Sports
Grammar: present simple, adverbs of frequency, *love/like/hate* + *-ing*, prepositions of time
Everyday English: Making arrangements
Writing: A blog entry about your typical Sunday

Vocabulary

Daily routines

1 Look at the pictures. 🎧 Listen and learn.

In the morning

12:00 midnight–12:00 noon

1. wake up early
2. have a shower
3. get dressed
4. have breakfast
5. catch the bus to college

At midday

12:00 noon

6. have a break for lunch

In the afternoon

12:00 noon–6:00 pm

7. finish college
8. go jogging

In the evening

6:00 pm–12:00 midnight

9. do homework
10. work part-time

11. go back home
12. chat with friends online

13. have dinner
14. go to bed

Reading

2 a) **Does Valeria go to work every morning?**
🎧 Listen and read to find out.

 VIDEO

1 Valeria López is 17 and she's a college student. She also works **part-time** at an animal shelter. "I really like my job because I love working with animals. My job is tiring, though, as I often work long hours. There's a lot to do in the shelter," she says.

2 Valeria wakes up at 6:30. She has a shower, gets dressed and then has breakfast. Around 7:15 am, Valeria catches the bus to college. Her lessons start at 7:45 am. She always has a **break** for lunch at noon. Valeria works at the shelter every Monday, Wednesday and Friday. From 5:00 pm to 9:00 pm, she shows visitors around the shelter and helps **care for** the animals that live there. She gets back home, has dinner and listens to music or Skypes her friends before she goes to bed at around 11:00. "I've got a busy routine but it's OK," Valeria says. "I am a hard-working person."

3 So, what does Valeria do in her free time? She likes going for long walks in the countryside with her dog, Max. She also loves playing basketball with her friends when she isn't at the shelter.

4 "I feel very **satisfied** with my life at the moment," says Valeria. "I love working at the shelter and I enjoy my free time. Who can ask for more?"

✓ **Check these words**

animal shelter, tiring, catch the bus, break, care for, walk, countryside, satisfied

b) (THINK) Think of a title for the text.

3 a) Read the text again and match the headings (A-E) to the paragraphs (1-4). One heading is extra.

A Happy with Life **D** A Working Student
B My Daily Routine **E** Fun Time
C A Normal College Day

b) Decide if the sentences are *T* (True) or *F* (False). Then, explain the words in bold.

1 Valeria gets up early. ....
2 She walks to college. ....
3 She goes to the shelter every day. ....
4 She has got a dog. ....

Speaking
Telling the time

We tell the **time** in **two** different ways

 six o'clock **OR** six
 half past six **OR** six thirty

 (a) quarter to six **OR** five forty-five
 (a) quarter past six **OR** six fifteen

 twenty to six **OR** five forty
 twenty past six **OR** six twenty

Note: *am: before midday*
pm: after midday

4 Look at the clock faces. Ask and answer questions, as in the example. Tell the time in both ways.

a b c

d e

f g h i

A: What time is it? *A: What's the time?*
B: It's (a) quarter to seven. *B: It's six forty-five.*

Days of the week

5 Listen and learn. Which days are weekdays?

Monday Wednesday Friday Sunday
Tuesday Thursday Saturday

Listening

6 Listen to Tony's weekday daily routine and make notes under these headings: *In the morning – At noon – In the afternoon – In the evening*. Present his routine to the class.

7 What is your daily routine like? Tell the class. Use the headings in Ex. 6 to help you.

Writing (an email)

8 You and your family now live in a new country. Write an email to your English-speaking friend about your typical weekday. Write what you do in the *morning, afternoon* and *evening* (50-80 words).

INBOX

Hi ...!
Hope you're well. Life here is great. In the morning, I wake up at ... . In the afternoon, I ... . In the evenings, I ... .
What do you usually do every day?
Write back,
...

Grammar in Use

Mary: Hi Kim, do you know where Lucy is? I need to give her a book.

Kim: I'm not sure. She usually eats in the cafeteria at noon. She likes spending her break there.

Mary: Well, I don't think she's there. It's never open after 2:30. What time does she leave college?

Kim: On Thursdays, she has football practice with the college team, so she always leaves quite early, at four o'clock. Why don't you drop it off at her flat on your way home?

Mary: Does she live near here?

Kim: Yes, she does. She lives at number 14, Elm Park.

Mary: OK. Thanks Kim.

1 Study the theory. Find examples in the dialogue.

Present Simple

Affirmative

I/You work.	He/She/It works.	We/You/They work.

Use:
We use the present simple for:
- **permanent states**. *He lives in Madrid.*
- **repeated actions**. *I go to the gym every afternoon.*
- **daily routines**. *I brush my teeth in the morning.*

Form:
- Most verbs take an **-s** in the affirmative third person singular. *I work – he works*
- Verbs ending in **-ss**, **-sh**, **-ch**, **-x**, **-o** take **-es**. *you finish – she finishes*
- Verbs ending in **consonant + -y** drop the **-y** and take **-ies**. *we study – he studies* **BUT:** *I play – she plays*

2 Fill in the third-person singular.

1 I go – he ....
2 I work – he ....
3 I love – he ....

4 I wash – he ....
5 I fly – he ....
6 I enjoy – he ....

3 Put the verbs in brackets into the present simple.

1 Mary *leaves* **(leave)** the house at 8 o'clock in the morning.

2 She .... **(catch)** the bus to college with her friends Mia and Darren.

3 Mary's mother .... **(work)** in a hospital; she's a nurse.

4 Mary .... **(finish)** her lessons at 3:30.

5 Mary's dad .... **(go)** home at 4:00 pm every day.

6 Mary .... **(tidy)** her bedroom in the afternoon.

7 After she has dinner with her parents, Mary .... **(watch)** TV.

8 Mary .... **(have)** a busy daily routine but her weekends are great.

9 Every Saturday, Mary .... **(meet)** her friends at the mall.

10 She .... **(like)** going to the cinema on Saturday evenings.

4 Study the table. Find examples in the dialogue. How do we form the present simple negative?

Present Simple

Negative	
Long form	**Short form**
I/You **do not** work.	I/You **don't** work.
He/She/It **does not** work.	He/She/It **doesn't** work.
We/You/They **do not** work.	We/You/They **don't** work.

Interrogative	Short answers	
Do I/you work?	**Yes**, I/you **do**.	**No**, I/you **don't**.
Does he/she/it work?	**Yes**, he/she/it **does**.	**No**, he/she/it **doesn't**.
Do we/you/they work?	**Yes**, we/you/they **do**.	**No**, we/you/they **don't**.

5 Fill in *do*, *does*, *don't* or *doesn't*.

1 "*Do* you play football?" "Yes, I *do*."

2 ".................... your friend live in that house?" "Yes, he ...."

3 ".................... Vicky like basketball?" "No, she ...."

4 "................. you like rock music?" "Yes, I ...."

5 "What time .... Karen start work?" "Sorry, I .... know."

6 "................. you eat lunch at work?" "No, I ...."

7 "................. they walk to school?" "No, they ...."

6 **a)** **Study the theory. Find examples in the dialogue on p. 32.**

Adverbs of frequency

never 0%	sometimes 50%	usually 90%
rarely 5%	often 70%	always 100%

Adverbs of frequency usually come:
- before the main verb. *I **usually** get up early in the morning.*
- after the verb **to be**. *I am **never** late for work.*
- after auxiliary verbs. *I don't **often** have lunch at noon.*

b) **Which of the following do you** *never/rarely/ sometimes/often/usually/always* **do on Sundays?**

- have football practice • go jogging • meet friends
- go to the cinema • play basketball • eat out
- watch TV • cook dinner • chat with friends online

I never have football practice on Sundays.

7 SPEAKING **Ask and answer questions, as in the example. Then, write a short paragraph about your partner.**

How often do you ...
go swimming?
go to the theatre?
cook?
go for long walks?
go out with your family?
play computer games?
watch TV?
meet your friends?

- never, often, etc.
- every day/month/ evening, etc.
- every two/three days/Sunday, etc.
- once/twice/three times a week/ month, etc.

A: *How often do you go swimming?*
B: *Twice a week.*

Tony goes swimming twice a week and ...

8 **a)** **Study the theory. Find an example in the dialogue on p. 32.**

love/like/hate + -ing

We use the **-ing form** after the verbs:
love (✓✓)   **like** (✓)   **don't like** (✗)   **hate** (✗✗)

*I **love** play**ing** football and I **like** listen**ing** to music. I **don't like** watch**ing** TV, though.*
OR
*I **love** play**ing** football and I **like** listen**ing** to music, but I **don't like** watch**ing** TV.*

b) **Complete the sentences. Use:** *like (✓), love (✓✓), don't like (✗), hate (✗✗)* **and the verbs:** *listen, go, watch, wake up, play.*

1 I *love playing* (✓✓) basketball with my brother.
2 My mum .... (✓) to pop music.
3 My dad .... (✗✗) to the cinema.
4 My sister Anna .... (✗) early.
5 My granddad .... (✓✓) TV in the afternoon.

c) SPEAKING **What do you** *like/love/don't like/ hate* **doing? Tell your partner.**

9 **Study the theory. Find examples in the dialogue on p. 32.**

Prepositions of time

- We use **at** in the expressions: *at the weekend, at noon, at midday, at midnight, at night;* with the time: *at six o'clock*
- We use **on** with days of the week: *on Monday;* in the expression: *on weekdays;* with parts of a particular day: *on Sunday morning(s);* with dates: *on 2nd August*
- We use **in** with months & seasons: *in January, in summer;* in the expressions: *in the morning, in the afternoon, in the evening*

10 **Fill in** *at, in* **or** *on.* **Compare Henry's routine to your teacher's.**

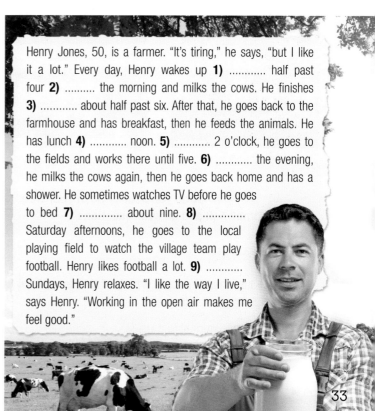

Henry Jones, 50, is a farmer. "It's tiring," he says, "but I like it a lot." Every day, Henry wakes up **1)** .... half past four **2)** .... the morning and milks the cows. He finishes **3)** .... about half past six. After that, he goes back to the farmhouse and has breakfast, then he feeds the animals. He has lunch **4)** .... noon. **5)** .... 2 o'clock, he goes to the fields and works there until five. **6)** .... the evening, he milks the cows again, then he goes back home and has a shower. He sometimes watches TV before he goes to bed **7)** .... about nine. **8)** .... Saturday afternoons, he goes to the local playing field to watch the village team play football. Henry likes football a lot. **9)** .... Sundays, Henry relaxes. "I like the way I live," says Henry. "Working in the open air makes me feel good."

33

Skills in Action

Vocabulary
Free-time activities

1 a) 🎧 **Look at the pictures. Listen and learn.**

listen to music

read a book

go dancing

go on a picnic

go to the mall

go to the cinema

visit museums

meet friends

watch a film

do yoga

play football

go to the library

b) 🗣️🗣️ **What do you usually do in your free time? Ask and answer questions.**

Listening

2 🎧 **Listen and decide which of the sentences are _T_ (True) or _F_ (False).**

1 Ann loves listening to music. ....
2 Holly doesn't like reading. ....
3 Ann likes going to the mall. ....
4 Holly and Ann both like visiting museums. ....

Everyday English
Making arrangements

3 🗣️🗣️ **These phrases are from a dialogue between two friends. What is the dialogue about?** 🎧 **Listen and read to find out.**

- Are you free this Saturday? • I think so. Why?
- Do you want to ...? • Sure. What time do you want to meet? • Can we meet at a different time? • No problem. Let's meet at ... • See you there.

Harry:	Hey Tom, are you free this Saturday?
Tom:	I think so. Why?
Harry:	Do you want to go swimming with me?
Tom:	Sure. What time do you want to meet?
Harry:	Is half past two good for you?
Tom:	Not really. My drama class doesn't finish until three o'clock. Can we meet at a different time?
Harry:	No problem. Let's meet at the swimming pool at quarter to four, then. Don't be late.
Tom:	OK, 3:45 sounds good to me. See you there.

4 **Find phrases in the dialogue which mean:**

- I'm afraid not. • Probably. • Meet you there.
- Make sure you're on time.

5 🗣️🗣️ **Arrange to meet your partner. Act out a dialogue similar to the one in Ex. 3. Use phrases from the language box. Use the following ideas.**

- this Monday / go to the cinema
- this Friday / visit the new modern art museum

Suggesting	Agreeing/Disagreeing
• Are you free ...?	• Sure.
• Do you want to ...?	• Yes, why not?
• How about + (-_ing_ form) ...?	• I'd love to.
• Let's + (inf. without _to_)	....
• We can	• Not really.
	• I'm afraid I can't.
	• I'm afraid not.

Pronunciation /s/ /z/ /ɪz/

6 🎧 **Listen and tick (✓). Listen again and repeat.**

	/s/	/z/	/ɪz/		/s/	/z/	/ɪz/
lives				writes			
walks				washes			
goes				watches			

Reading & Writing

Study Skills

Completing a text

Read the text quickly to understand what it is about. Read the text again and pay attention to the words before and after each gap. Think of what type of word is missing (noun, verb, preposition etc.). When you finish, read the text again and check if it makes sense.

7 a) **Read the blog and complete the missing words. What type of word is each?**

Christy's blog

Dad Sunday

Everyone loves Sunday, but I have a special reason. You see, Sunday is my day **1)** .... Dad! I always wake up very early **2)** .... cycle over to his flat for breakfast. **3)** .... the morning, we often go by bike to a farmer's market to get fresh food for lunch. Dad's **4)** .... amazing cook! In the afternoon, **5)** .... usually go to the city centre and visit a museum or **6)** .... art gallery. In the evening, we sometimes go to the cinema or stay at home and relax. I love my Dad Sundays! How **7)** .... you spend your Sundays?

b)  **Listen and check.**

Writing Tip

Opening/Closing remarks in blog entries

We can start/end a blog entry with one of the following techniques:

- **Offer a general thought** (*Sundays are great.*)
- **Address the reader directly** (*How do you feel about the weekend?*)
- **Ask a rhetorical question** (*I really enjoy Sundays, but who doesn't?*)

8 **Read the *Writing Tip* box. What technique does Christy use to start/end her blog entry?**

Writing (a blog entry about your typical Sunday)

Study Skills

Brainstorming

Before you start writing, read the rubric, underline the key words, then brainstorm for words/ideas related to the topic. This will help you do the task.

9 **Read the rubric. Look at the underlined key words and then brainstorm for words/ideas under the headings below.**

Write a reply to Christy's blog in Ex. 7 (60-80 words). Write:
- what <u>you usually do</u> on a <u>typical Sunday</u>.
- who with.
- how you like it.

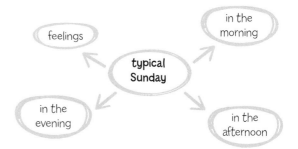

feelings — typical Sunday — in the morning — in the evening — in the afternoon

10 **Use your notes in Ex. 9 to write your blog entry. Follow the plan.**

Plan

Title
- introduce the topic
- what you usually do in the morning/afternoon/evening
- comments/feelings

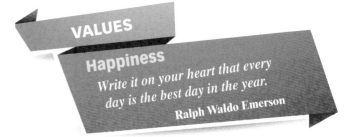

VALUES

Happiness

Write it on your heart that every day is the best day in the year.

Ralph Waldo Emerson

▶ VIDEO

Hobbies & Sports
Australia VS Canada

There are lots of exciting ways to enjoy your free time. In Australia and Canada sport is an important part of life.

People in Australia love swimming. They often take part in surfing and ocean swimming competitions like the Aussies — an annual sports competition. They also love team sports like Australian football, rugby and cricket.

People in Canada enjoy snowboarding, skiing, curling, rugby, cricket and baseball. Ice hockey is Canada's official winter sport and lacrosse is their official summer sport.

Playing sports and enjoying your free time are important all over the world. But these countries really are sports mad!

snowboarding 9

skiing 8

surfing 7

baseball 1

cricket 2

lacrosse 3

rugby 4

curling 5

ice hockey 6

✓ **Check these words**

take part, competition, annual, official

Listening & Reading

1 🎧 **Look at the pictures. Listen and learn. Do you/your friends do any of these sports? Which sport is your favourite?**

2 **Which of these sports are popular in:** *Australia*? *Canada*?
🎧 **Listen and read to find out.**

Speaking & Writing

3 THINK **Compare and contrast the sports people play in these two countries.**

4 ICT 👥 **What sports are popular in your country? Collect information, then write a short text for the class English magazine.**

Vocabulary

1 **Fill in:** *get*, *have*, *wake*, *chat*, *catch* **in the correct form.**

1 In the morning, Andrea .... up at 7 o'clock.

2 At half past seven, she .... dressed.

3 Then, she .... a big breakfast.

4 She always .... the eight-o'clock bus.

5 She .... with her friend Angie online before dinner.

(5 x 2 = 10)

2 **Write the time in two different ways.**

1 **6:00** *It's six o'clock. It's six.*

2 **8:30** ....

3 **5:45** ....

4 **9:15** ....

5 **2:40** ....

6 **4:25** ....

(5 x 2 = 10)

3 **Fill in:** *listen*, *read*, *go (x3)*, *visit*, *watch*, *do*, *play*, *meet*.

1 .... a book

2 .... a museum

3 .... friends

4 .... football

5 .... a film

6 .... yoga

7 .... snorkelling

8 .... dancing

9 .... to music

10 .... on a picnic

(10 x 2 = 20)

Grammar

4 **Put the verbs in the *present simple* and the adverbs of frequency in the correct place.**

1 Mandy .... **(work/always)** from 9 to 5.

2 Alan .... **(be/usually)** on time for class.

3 The children .... **(play/often)** at the park.

4 Mum .... **(wash/sometimes)** the dishes.

5 Mark .... **(tidy/never)** his room on Sundays.

(5 x 2 = 10)

5 **Fill in:** *do*, *does*, *don't*, *doesn't*.

1 "........... Mark like basketball?" "Yes, he ...."

2 "........... your parents work as vets?" "No, they ...."

3 ".............. Mary live near college?" "No, she ...."

4 ".............. you go home at 7 pm?" "Yes, I ...."

5 "............... the kids have dinner at 7:30?" "Yes, they ...."

(5 x 2 = 10)

6 **Fill in:** *in*, *on*, *at*.

1 I play volleyball .... the weekend.

2 My sister has a break for lunch .... noon.

3 .... Fridays, I usually meet my friends.

4 We like going swimming .... the summer.

5 Steve comes back .... 7th March.

(5 x 2 = 10)

7 **Complete the sentences. Use:** *like (✓)*, *love (✓✓)*, *not like (x)*, *hate (xx)* **and the verbs:** *go (x2)*, *chat*, *clean*, *have* **in the correct form.**

1 I .... (✓✓) lunch in the cafeteria with my friends.

2 My mum .... (✓) to the library in her free time.

3 Jenny .... (xx) her room without any help.

4 Kevin .... (✓) with his friends online.

5 My dad .... (x) to the cinema.

(5 x 2 = 10)

Everyday English

8 **Match the exchanges.**

1 ☐ Are you free this Sunday?

2 ☐ Do you want to play football with me?

3 ☐ Is ten to two good for you?

4 ☐ What's the time, please?

5 ☐ How often do you swim?

A Not really. Can we meet at 3?

B Twice a week.

C I think so. Why?

D Sure.

E It's half past one.

(5 x 4 = 20)

Total 100

Competences

GOOD ✓

VERY GOOD ✓✓

EXCELLENT ✓✓✓

Lexical Competence

Talk about
• daily routines
• free-time activities
• days of the week
• the time
• sports

Reading Competence

• identify the main idea of a paragraph (match headings to paragraphs)
• read for detail (T/F statements)

Listening Competence

• listen for specific information (T/F statements)

Speaking Competence

• make arrangements

Writing Competence

• write an email about my daily routine
• write a blog entry about my typical Sunday

Vocabulary: Wild animals, Parts of animals' bodies, Farm animals
Grammar: modal verbs: *can/could* (making/granting requests – asking for/giving permission), *can't* (refusing requests/permission), *must* (obligation), *mustn't* (prohibition), question words

Everyday English: Asking for information
Writing: Filling in a form to volunteer

Birds of a feather

▶ VIDEO

HOME | ABOUT US | SEA KAYAKING TOURS | WILDLIFE | CONTACT US

Home > Wildlife

Welcome to
Pohatu Marine Reserve

Here at Pohatu in Akaroa, New Zealand we protect dolphins and penguins. We also offer sea kayak tours along the coast. There, you can see these wonderful animals up close and learn more about them!

Dolphins

Dolphins are mammals. They have babies and feed them on milk. Dolphins are not fish, but they live in water. They can swim very well. They haven't got legs. They've got grey skin and a big **smile**. They've also got fins and a tail to help them swim. They **weigh** from seventy to five hundred kilos.

Dolphins are very **intelligent** animals. They can **easily** learn how to play games and are **friendly** to people.

Dolphins live in warm seas in many different parts of the world. They live in small groups and they eat fish. They live for about fifty years.

Penguins

Penguins **lay eggs** and they've got small wings, so they are like other birds, but they can't fly! They can swim very well, though. They are black and white, and they've got very short legs and a short tail. They've also got **thick** feathers to keep them **warm** in cold water. They weigh about twenty kilos.

Penguins look **funny** when they walk. However, when they are in the water, they swim like fish.

Penguins live on the ice of Antarctica and in the seas around it. They live in big groups and they eat fish. They live for about twenty years.

Click here to find out more

✓ **check these words**

coast, feed on, fin, weigh, warm, lay eggs, thick, ice

Reading

1 Read these sentences and decide if they are *T* (True) or *F* (False). What is the purpose of the text?
🎧 Listen and read to find out.

1 Dolphins are fish. ....
2 Dolphins live in groups. ....
3 Penguins weigh about thirty kilos. ....
4 Penguins live in Antarctica. ....

2 Read again and answer the questions. Then explain the words in bold.

1 What can dolphins do very well?
2 Where do dolphins live?
3 How long do dolphins live?
4 Why are penguins unusual birds?
5 What have penguins got to keep them warm?

Speaking

3 Copy and complete the table. Use your notes to compare the two animals.

	Dolphins	Penguins
kind of animal:	*mammals*	
unusual because:		
they can:		
they've got:		
they weigh:		
they live:		
they eat:		
they live for:		

Dolphins are mammals. ...

Vocabulary
Wild animals

Study Skills

Learning new words
Associate words with pictures. This helps you remember them.

4 Look at the pictures.
🎧 Listen and learn.

zebra

bear

crocodile

giraffe

flamingo

onkey

elephant

snake

5 Find the definitions of *mammals*, *birds*, *reptiles*, in your dictionary. Classify the animals in Ex. 4.

Elephants are mammals.

Parts of animals' bodies

6 Use the words below to label the parts of the animals' bodies. Check in your dictionary.

• beak • feathers • tail • paws • fur • neck

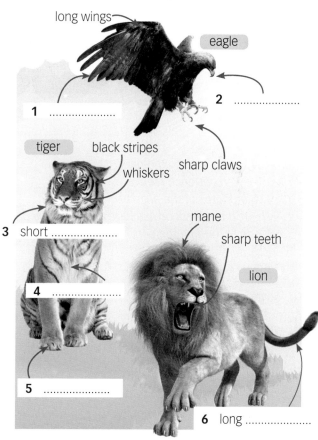

long wings

eagle

1 ....

2 ....

tiger   black stripes

whiskers   sharp claws

3 short ....

mane

sharp teeth

lion

4 ....

5 ....

6 long ....

Speaking

7 a) Which of the animals in Ex. 4 have got …

• thick fur? • a short tail? • a big mouth? • a long neck? • very big ears? • a long body? • feathers? • wings? • claws? • long legs? • a trunk?

b) Choose an animal in Ex. 4 and describe it to the class.

8 **THINK** Which is your favourite animal? Why?

Writing (a fact file about an animal)

9 **ICT** Use the headings in Ex. 3 to collect information about an animal in Ex. 4. Write a short text about it.

Grammar in Use

Explore 1,800 acres of wildlife preserve, home to over 3,500 animals across 260 species from six continents of the world. Visitors:

- *MUSTN'T bring pets to the park.*
- *MUST pay an entrance fee.*
- *CAN take photos of the animals.*
- *CAN bring their own food and have a picnic in the park.*
- *CAN'T drive through the park.*

FAQ

Q: Where is the Safari Park?
A: *35 miles northeast of the zoo, in Escondido, California.*

Q: When is the park open?
A: *Visitors can come any day between 9:00 am and 5:00 pm.*

Q: How much does a ticket cost?
A: *Tickets cost $52 for adults, but are free for children under 3.*

1 Study the theory. Find examples on the San Diego Zoo Safari Park webpage.

Modal verbs: *must/mustn't, can/can't/could*

- We use **must** to express **obligation/duty**.
  Visitors to the zoo must follow the rules. (They are obliged to.)
- We use **mustn't** to express **prohibition**.
  You mustn't disturb the animals. (It's forbidden.)
- We use *can* to **make/grant a request** or to **ask for/give permission**. (informal)
  Can I go to the aquarium later, Mum? Of course you can. (informal)
  COMPARE: *Could I see the manager? Yes, you can.* (NOT: ~~Yes, you could.~~) formal (Is it OK for me to ...?)
  Can we take photographs here, Dad? Yes, you can. (Do we have permission to ...?)
- We use *can't* to **refuse a request/permission**.
  I'm afraid you can't feed the monkeys now. (It's not OK.)
  You can't enter this area. (You don't have permission.)

2 🎧 Listen to a man telling some new shark tank cleaners the rules of cleaning tanks. Tick (✓) the correct box. Then write sentences using *must* or *mustn't*, as in the example.

Shark tank cleaners	must	mustn't
work alone		✓
enter a tank with sharks in it		
clean tanks after meals		
do over 1,000 dives per year		
stay in the water very long		
use strong soap		

Shark tank cleaners mustn't work alone.

3 Fill in: *must or mustn't.*

1 You .... feed the animals.
2 You .... pay to park here.
3 You .... smoke here.
4 You .... keep the zoo clean.

4 👥 Ask and answer questions, as in the example. Use *can/can't*, or *could*.

1 Ask your mum if you can have a sandwich. (✓)
   A: *Can I have a sandwich?*
   B: *Yes, you can.*
2 Ask the zookeeper if you can pick up a snake. (✗)
3 Ask your manager for permission to go home early. (✓)
4 Ask your friend to borrow his camera. (✗)
5 Ask your friend for permission to open the window. (✓)
6 Ask for permission to drive through the safari park. (✗)

5 What *can/can't/must/mustn't* you do at college/home?

6 Study the table. Find examples on the San Diego Zoo Safari Park webpage in Ex. 1.

Question words

We use question words to ask about different kinds of information:

What does it eat? *(things)* Tree leaves and grass.
Where does it live? *(place)* In the forests of Africa.
When does it sleep? *(time)* At night.
Why does it have stripes? *(reason)* Because they help it hide.
How long is its tongue? *(length)* About 45 cm long.
How tall is it? *(height)* About 1.5 metres.
How much does it weigh? *(quantity)* Between 200 and 300 kg.
How long does it live for? *(time)* Twenty to thirty years.
How many okapis are there in the wild? *(number/ quantity)* About 25,000.

7 Complete the gaps. Use: *where, when, how many, how long, how much, why, what (x2)*.

Insect Facts

1 A: *What* colour are ladybirds?
B: Yellow, red or orange with black spots on their wings.

2 A: .... do caterpillars live for?
B: Just a few weeks.

3 A: .... legs have centipedes got?
B: They've got 28 to 354 legs.

4 A: .... do ants live?
B: Under the ground.

5 A: .... do cockroaches weigh?
B: About 30g.

6 A: .... do dragonflies hunt for food?
B: In the summer months.

7 A: .... are butterflies very colourful?
B: Because their colours help them hide.

8 A: .... do praying mantises eat?
B: Other insects.

8 Form questions to which the underlined words are the answers.

Kangaroos are mammals. They have babies and feed them on <u>milk</u>. They live in <u>Australia</u>. They are about <u>two metres tall</u> and weigh about <u>sixty kilos</u>. Kangaroos have got <u>two</u> back legs, two short front legs and a long tail. <u>They can jump very high</u> because their back legs are very strong. They sleep <u>during the day</u> and they eat <u>leaves</u>. Kangaroos carry their babies in a <u>pouch</u>. They live in small groups. They live for <u>fifteen to twenty years</u>.

What do kangaroos feed their babies on? (milk)

9 **SPEAKING** Use the prompts to ask and answer questions about the animals below.

1
- … this animal? sea lion
- … weigh? about 250 kilos
- … eat? fish
- … can/do? swim very well
- … live? Pacific Ocean
- … live? about 15 years

2
- … this animal? tiger
- … weigh? about 200 kilos
- … eat? deer and monkeys
- … sleep? during the day
- … live? forests in India
- … live? about 15 years

10 **ICT** Collect information about various mammals, birds and reptiles, and create a quiz. Swap with another group.

Skills in Action

| **1** rooster | **2** turkey | **3** cow | **4** duck | **5** horse | **6** goose | **7** donkey | **8** hen | **9** sheep | **10** goat |

Vocabulary
Farm animals

1 🎧 Look at the pictures. Listen and learn.

Listening

2 🎧 Listen to the dialogue and decide if the statements (1-6) are *T* (True) or *F* (False).

1 Matt lives on a farm. ....
2 Rocky and Blaze are the same age. ....
3 The horses' favourite food is carrots. ....
4 Matt feeds his horses once a day. ....
5 Matt cleans the stables once every week. ....
6 Matt doesn't mind looking after his horses. ....

3 👤👤 Study the sizes, then read the examples. In pairs, ask and answer questions about the animals in Ex. 1, as in the example.

What is this animal?   *It's a donkey.*
What colour is it?   *It's brown.*
How big is it?   *It's very big.*
How big are its ears?   *They're quite big.*
How long is its tail?   *It's quite long.*

Everyday English
Asking for information

4 Read the first and the last exchange in the dialogue. What is it about? When is Tony free?

🎧 Listen and read to find out.

Lucy:	Good afternoon. How can I help?
Tony:	Hello, I'm interested in volunteering at the farm.
Lucy:	That's great. What's your name?
Tony:	Tony Morgan.
Lucy:	I'm Lucy Stevens, the farm manager. When are you available?
Tony:	I'm free on Saturday mornings.
Lucy:	Can you also come on Sunday afternoons?
Tony:	I'm afraid I can't. I work part-time at a café.
Lucy:	Oh OK! When can you start?
Tony:	This Saturday if it's OK with you.
Lucy:	Perfect! Come at 9:00 and ask for Steve.
Tony:	Thanks.

5 👤👤 You want to volunteer at an animal shelter. Take roles and act out a dialogue similar to the one in Ex. 4.

Asking for information	Giving information
• What's your name? • When are you available? • Can you also come on ...?	• I'm ... . • I'm free on ... . • Yes, I can./I'm afraid I can't.

Pronunciation /e/ /ɜ:/

6 🎧 Listen and repeat.

/e/ leg, head
/ɜ:/ bird, fur

Reading & Writing

7 Look at the form below. What kind of form is it? Who writes it? Why? Read to find out.

VOLUNTEER APPLICATION FORM

1 [_____]

Title (Mr/~~Mrs~~/~~Miss~~/~~Ms~~) **& Name:** Michael Dawson

Address: 5 Huckleberry Lane, Pilton, Somerset

Postcode: BA24 7DP

Telephone 01963 766 122   **Mobile** 07700900817

Email: m.dawson@email.com

Age: ☐ 16-17 yrs   ☑ 18-24 yrs   ☐ 25+ yrs

2 [_____]

Education:
- A levels in Chemistry and English
- now in second year of university studying Physics

Volunteering experience:
- three months working in a dog hotel
- two weeks at an animal rescue centre

Skills: I can drive a car and I know first aid.

3 [_____]

☐ **full-time**   ☐ **part-time**   ☐ **retired**

☐ **unemployed** ☑ **student**

4 [_____]

Please tick boxes as appropriate.

☐ **dog walking**   ☑ **cat care**

☐ **charity shop**   ☐ **helping hands**

☑ **other** (please say what) I am also interested in doing fundraising events.

5 [_____]

I am available Mondays 5 to 8 pm and Sundays 12 to 5 pm.

Signature: *Michael Dawson*

8 a) Complete the gaps (1-5) in the form with the correct headings (A-E).

A PRESENT EMPLOYMENT
B AVAILABILITY
C PERSONAL DETAILS
D INTERESTS
E STUDIES; EXPERIENCE

b) ⟨**THINK**⟩ Imagine you are a manager at an animal charity. Do you think Michael Dawson is a good applicant? Why (not)?

Writing Tip

Completing application forms

When we fill in application forms, we usually give the information in a number of different ways. That is:
- tick boxes to choose options.
- write in note form to give brief details.
- write in full sentences to explain something.

9 Look at the completed application form in Ex. 7. How many full sentences does the writer use? How does he present the other information? Give examples.

Writing (an application form to volunteer)

10 You have some free time and you want to volunteer at an animal shelter. Copy the application form in Ex. 7 in your notebook. Use the headings in Ex. 8a to fill in a volunteer application form.

VALUES

Volunteering

When you give yourself, you receive more than you give.

(Antoine de Saint-Exupery)

▶ **VIDEO**

UNIQUE animals

Australia is home to a lot of animals that you can't find anywhere else in the world. Here are just some of the unique animals that live in Australia's outback.

A **Emus** can't fly, but they can run very fast – up to 48 kilometres per hour. These huge birds lay around 50 eggs each year. These eggs are green so they are not easy to see on the ground. The male emu looks after them.

B Go anywhere in Australia and you are sure to find **kangaroos** in grasslands. They've got thick fur and hop around using their big feet and strong tails. They keep their babies in a pouch, a pocket on their stomach.

C In the trees of Australia there are cute **koalas**. They've got fluffy ears and fur, and a nose that looks like a spoon. They only eat eucalyptus leaves.

D In the rivers of Australia there is a very strange creature. It's got a duck's bill on its face, the tail of a beaver and the feet of an otter. It's a **platypus** and it's one of the few mammals that lays eggs.

✓ **Check these words**

ground, male, fluffy, spoon, eucalyptus, bill, beaver, otter

Listening & Reading

1 Look at the pictures. Where are these animals from? What is special about them?
🎧 Listen and read to find out.

2 Read the texts again. Which animal (A, B, C or D) ...

looks like three different animals?	1	☐
can move very quickly?	2	☐
carries their young around with them?	3	☐
lives on only one kind of food?	4	☐

Speaking & Writing

3 Tell the class one thing that you find interesting about each animal.

4 **ICT** 🐾 What unique animals are there in your country? In groups, collect information. Write a short text for an international nature magazine or prepare a digital presentation. Use pictures.

Vocabulary

1 **Match the animals to their descriptions.**

1	☐ It's got a long trunk.	A	kangaroo
2	☐ It's got stripes.	B	lion
3	☐ It's got a mane.	C	tiger
4	☐ There's a big fin on its back.	D	elephant
5	☐ It's got pink feathers.	E	dolphin
6	☐ It's got a pouch.	F	flamingo

(6 x 1 = 6)

2 **Fill in:** *claws, mouths, fur, neck, stripes.*

1 A zebra's black and white .... help it to hide.
2 Big birds use their .... to catch small animals.
3 Koalas are cute animals with thick grey ....
4 A giraffe has a long .... to reach its food.
5 Sharks have huge .... full of sharp teeth.

(5 x 2 = 10)

3 **Complete the sentences.**

1 Snakes are r _ _ _ _ _ _ _ .
2 Lions have got thick m _ _ _ _ .
3 Donkeys aren't wild animals; they are f _ _ _ animals.
4 Bears are m _ _ _ _ _ _ .
5 Penguins have got w _ _ _ _ but they can't fly.

(5 x 2 = 10)

4 **Fill in with the correct form of the verbs:** *keep, lay, have, look, weigh.*

The Arctic fox lives in very cold places like Russia and Canada. It has got lots of fur to **1)** .... it warm. It has a long body and tail, and can **2)** .... up to ten kilos. It's a mammal so it doesn't **3)** .... eggs. During the spring months, it **4)** .... babies, usually between five and nine of them. The Arctic fox is a beautiful animal. It **5)** .... very funny, too, when it dives deep into the snow to catch its food.

(5 x 4 = 20)

Grammar

5 **Complete the exchanges with:** *can, can't, could, must* **or** *mustn't.*

1 A: Mum, ... I have a glass of milk, please?
   B: Yes, of course you ....
2 A: .... we feed the monkeys, sir?
   B: I'm afraid not. You .... feed the monkeys – it's forbidden.
3 A: We .... be quiet in the wildlife park.
   B: Yes, it says so at the entrance. We .... make a noise!

(6 x 3 = 18)

6 **Fill in the correct question word.**

1 .... is this animal? An elephant.
2 .... does it live? In Africa and India.
3 .... is its trunk? About 2 metres.
4 .... does it weigh? About 4,000 kilos.
5 .... does it live for? About 60 years.
6 .... can it walk long distances? Because it's got strong legs.
7 .... legs has it got? Four.
8 .... does it sleep? At night.

(8 x 2 = 16)

Everyday English

7 **Match the exchanges.**

1	☐ How can I help?	A	OK. Thanks.
2	☐ When are you free?	B	I'm sorry, I can't.
3	☐ Can you come in on Sundays?	C	This Saturday.
4	☐ When can you start?	D	On Saturdays.
5	☐ Come at 10 am and ask for Adam.	E	I want to volunteer at the zoo.

(5 x 4 = 20)

Total 100

Competences

GOOD ✓
VERY GOOD ✓ ✓
EXCELLENT ✓ ✓ ✓

Lexical Competence
Talk about
• wild animals
• parts of animals' bodies
• farm animals

Reading Competence
• read for specific information (answer questions based on a text)
• read for detail (T/F statements; multiple matching)

Listening Competence
• listen for specific information (T/F statements)

Speaking Competence
• ask for information
• describe an animal

Writing Competence
• write a fact file of an animal
• fill in a volunteer application form

Come rain or shine

Vocabulary: Weather, Seasons, Months, Activities, Clothes
Grammar: Present continuous, Present continuous vs Present simple
Everyday English: Shopping for clothes
Writing: A postcard

Vocabulary

Weather, Months & Seasons

1 Look at the photos. In which photo is the weather: *rainy, cloudy and windy*? *freezing cold and snowy*? *cold and foggy*? *warm and sunny*?

A

Alenka

Kate

B

Mark

D

C

Laura

Nancy

2 Match the sentences to the photos in Ex. 1.

1 There are clouds in the sky and the wind is **blowing**. It's **raining**. It's a **rainy** day.
2 The sun is **shining**. It's sunny.
3 It's **snowing**. It's a **snowy** day.
4 There's **fog**. It's **foggy**.

3 a) Fill in the missing months.

> January – F................ – M................ – April –
> M.................. – June – J................... – August –
> September – O.................. – November –
> December

b) Which months are in the winter, spring, summer and autumn in your country?

4 👤👤 Ask and answer in pairs, as in the example.

A: *What's the weather like in summer?*
B: *It's warm and sunny ...*

Activities

5 a) Which photo shows someone who is ...

1 ☐ sailing a boat?
2 ☐ sightseeing?
3 ☐ holding an umbrella?
4 ☐ snowboarding?

b) Use the words/phrases in Exs 1-4 to describe the pictures.

In photo A it's foggy. Kate and Alenka are sightseeing.

Reading & Listening

6 🎧 Listen and match the weather to the places.

Weather	Places
1 ☐ It's freezing cold and snowy.	**A** Thailand
2 ☐ It's very hot and the sun is shining.	**B** Norway
3 ☐ It's windy, cold and raining.	**C** the Maldives

7 Read the text quickly. List all the words related to: *weather*; *clothes*.

Willis *in all* **Weathers**  VIDEO

Hi everyone! I'm Willis Weathers and today I'm visiting Trysil in Norway! Why am I wearing my heavy coat? It's **freezing cold** here! **In fact**, there's snow! Visitors are wearing hats and gloves. Some people are skiing, skating and snowboarding, but I just want to go **inside** and drink hot chocolate!

Willis Weathers is in beautiful Thailand today! I'm at an ancient temple and the weather here is a bit **strange**. It's warm, but it's raining! **Luckily**, I've got my umbrella with me. Some other tourists aren't so lucky – they're running to get out of the rain. At least these ladies behind me are wearing **waterproof** jackets!

Greetings from the Maldives! Willis Weathers here, and I'm warm and dry at last! The weather is fantastic today. It's very hot and the sun's shining. There isn't a cloud in the sky. People are sailing boats, swimming or playing volleyball on the golden **sand**. I love it here!

✓ **Check these words**

in fact, strange, waterproof jacket, sand

Study Skills

Reading for specific information

Read the statements and underline the key words. Find the part in the text that answers each question. Use the key words in the statement to decide if the statement is true or false, or if the text does not contain any information about it. Be careful. For a statement to be true, every part of the statement must be true.

8 Read the text again and decide if the statements (1-6) are *T* (true), *F* (false) or *DS* (doesn't say). Then explain the words in bold.

1 It's very cold in Norway. ....
2 People in Norway don't like hot weather. ....
3 It's raining in Thailand. ....
4 Willis thinks the temple is a bit strange. ....
5 It's cloudy in the Maldives. ....
6 Willis is happy to be in the Maldives. ....

Speaking

9 🎧 **Listen and read the text. Compare the weather in the three places.**

Writing (a blog post)

10 〔THINK〕 Imagine you are Willis Weathers. Write a blog post from your country reporting what the weather is like.

Grammar in Use

.ıll   09:37   ▭

< ✕

Hi Olivia! Are you doing anything special right now? Amelia and I aren't working today. We are planning a trip to the beach. Do you want to come with us? We usually go by bus, but today we're taking my brother's car. ☺ Do you want me to come and pick you up? Let me know ASAP.

>

1 **Study the theory. Complete the rule. Find examples in the text message.**

Present continuous	
Affirmative	**Negative**
I am play**ing** you are play**ing** he ⎫ she ⎬ is play**ing** it ⎭ we ⎫ you ⎬ are play**ing** they ⎭	I'm not play**ing** you aren't play**ing** he ⎫ she ⎬ isn't play**ing** it ⎭ we ⎫ you ⎬ aren't play**ing** they ⎭

To form the present continuous we use the verb **to be** and add .... to the base form of the main verb.
We use the present continuous for actions happening **now, at the moment of speaking**. We use this tense with *now*, **right now** and **at the moment**.
She's playing football now.
She isn't eating an ice cream at the moment.

Spelling
• Most verbs take **-ing** after the base form of the main verb.
 snow – snowing, wear – wearing
• Verbs ending in one stressed vowel and a consonant double the consonant and take **-ing**.
 stop – stopping, swim – swimming
• Verbs ending in **-e** drop the **-e** and take **-ing**.
 take – taking, decorate – decorating

2 **Add** *-ing* **to the following verbs.**

1	read	....	**7**	fish	....
2	sunbathe	....	**8**	ski	....
3	shine	....	**9**	buy	....
4	do	....	**10**	have	....
5	run	....	**11**	jog	....
6	make	....	**12**	visit	....

3 **Look at the pictures. Correct the sentences, as in the example. Use verbs from Ex. 2.**

1 Steve is eating an ice cream.
 No! Steve isn't eating an ice cream. He's jogging.
2 Ann is playing games on her mobile.
 ....
3 The dog is sleeping. ....
4 Peter is swimming. ....
5 Tom and Alex are having a barbecue.
 ....

4 **Put the verbs in brackets in the present continuous.**

Hi Abbie,
1) *I'm having* (have) a fantastic time here in Lisbon. The sun 2) .... (shine) and we 3) .... (enjoy) the warm weather a lot.
There are a lot of cafés and restaurants and the food is delicious. Today, we 4) .... (visit) Sintra, a beautiful town with lots of historic buildings very close to Lisbon. Your uncle 5) .... (buy) souvenirs at one of the shops here and Ben 6) .... (take) photos of the monuments.
It's so beautiful, I don't want to leave!
See you in two weeks,
Aunt Lily

Abbie Smith
12 Milles Street
London
NW1 7DN
UK

5 Study the table. How do we form the interrogative of the present continuous? Find examples in the text message on p. 48.

Present continuous

Interrogative	Short answers
Am I playing? Are you playing?	Yes, I am./No, I'm not. Yes, you are./No, you aren't.
Is he she it playing?	Yes, he/she/it is. No, he/she/it isn't.
Are we you they playing?	Yes, we/you/they are. No, we/you/they aren't.

6 Fill in: *am*, *is* or *are*, then complete the answers.

1 .... Sandy sleeping? No, ...
2 .... the kids doing their homework?
   Yes, ...
3 .... you having lunch? No, ...
4 .... he cooking? Yes, ...
5 .... I sitting here? No, ...
6 .... we having a meeting now?
   Yes, ...

7 🎧👥 First, listen to the sounds and tick (✓) what you hear. Then ask and answer questions, as in the example.

1 **Tony:** watch TV ☐   play tennis ✓
2 **Stella:** drive a car ☐   have a shower ☐
3 **Bob & Keith:** swim ☐   sleep ☐
4 **They:** listen to music ☐   play computer games ☐
5 **James:** ride a horse ☐   ride a motorbike ☐
6 **She:** play the guitar ☐   play the piano ☐
7 **They:** walk ☐   run ☐

A: *Is Tony watching TV?*
B: *No, he isn't. He's playing tennis.*

8 Read the examples and complete the rules. Find examples in the text message on p. 48.

Present continuous – Present simple

*John usually **wears** jeans and T-shirts.*
*John's **wearing** a suit and tie today.*

We use .... to talk about habits and daily routines.
We use .... to talk about actions happening now, at the moment of speaking.

9 Write sentences, as in the example.

Rita usually chat online on Sunday afternoon / study
Rita usually chats online on Sunday afternoon. Right now, she is studying.

Betty usually watch TV on Saturday morning / shop for clothes
....
....

James usually go jogging in the morning / ride his bike
....
....

[4] Ben usually listen to music in the afternoon / read a book
....
....

10 Put the verbs in brackets in the present simple or the present continuous.

Hi mate,
I'm in Denmark with Chris. We
1) .... (study) Geography here on an exchange programme. We 2) .... (stay) with my Danish friend Casper in Copenhagen. It's very cold here. It often 3) .... (rain), but right now it 4) .... (snow)! In the mornings, we 5) .... (go) to college. In the afternoons, we 6) .... (put on) our thick coats, hats and gloves and we 7) .... (walk) around the city. Life 8) .... (be) quiet here and the people 9) .... (be) quite friendly. Anyway, I've got to go – Casper 10) .... (make) hot chocolate. What about you? 11) .... (you/enjoy) your exchange programme? What 12) .... (you/do) there every day?
Write back,
Alfie

11 🔲WRITING 🗨THINK Write a reply to Alfie's email. Write about: *where you are – what the weather is like – what you do every day – what you are doing right now*.

Skills in Action

Vocabulary
Clothes

1 Look at the pictures. Complete the gaps. Use:
blouse, boots, scarf, trousers, cap, belt.

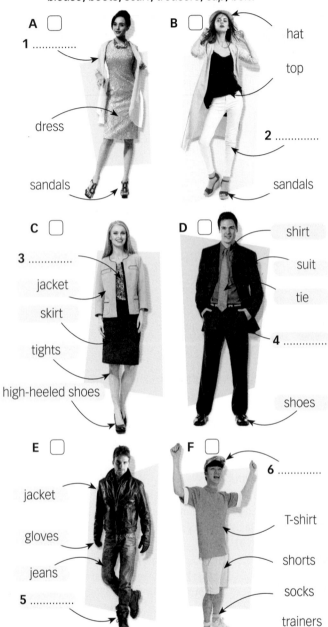

A ☐
1 ....
dress
sandals

B ☐
hat
top
2 ....
sandals

C ☐
3 ....
jacket
skirt
tights
high-heeled shoes

D ☐
shirt
suit
tie
4 ....
shoes

E ☐
jacket
gloves
jeans
5 ....

F ☐
6 ....
T-shirt
shorts
socks
trainers

Listening

2 a) Look at the pictures in Ex. 1.

🎧 Listen and number the pictures (A-F) as the designer describes each one.

b) Look at the pictures and describe each person's clothes.

3 GAME Choose a student in your class and describe his/her clothes. The first person to guess who you are describing goes next.

Everyday English
Shopping for clothes

4 a) Read the dialogue and complete the gaps.
🎧 Listen and check.

> **Sally** Hello, **1)** .... I help you?
> **Jack:** Hi, I'd like to return this jacket, please.
> **Sally:** Sure, what's wrong with it?
> **Jack:** I'm afraid it's too **2)** .... for me.
> **Sally:** I see. So we can give you a refund, or you can pick another item.
> **Jack:** Well, I like this jacket. **3)**.................... it in a bigger size?
> **Sally:** Let me check. **4)** .... size are you?
> **Jack:** I'm a large.
> **Sally:** I'm sorry, we only have medium in black. But we've got large in grey and red.
> **Jack:** Can I try the grey one, please?
> **Sally:** Sure. The fitting rooms are over here.

b) 👥 Use the clothes in the pictures to act out similar dialogues.

5 👥 Read the exchange. Use the pictures to act out similar exchanges.

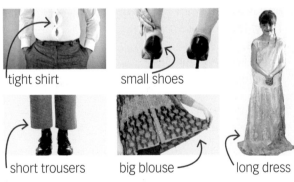

tight shirt   small shoes

short trousers   big blouse   long dress

A: What do you think of this shirt?
B: Well, I think it's too tight.

Pronunciation /n/ /ŋ/

6 🎧 Listen and tick (✓). Listen again and repeat.

	/n/	/ŋ/		/n/	/ŋ/
wearing			shine		
rain			fishing		
making			run		

Reading & Writing

7 Read the postcard and answer the questions.

1 Who is writing it?
2 Who is she sending it to?
3 Where is each person?

Hi Natalie,
Greetings from La Macarena, Colombia! The weather's lovely here. It's warm and sunny. We go sightseeing in the mornings with our group's guide. We taste different local foods every day and take lots of pictures. Today, we're visiting Caño Cristales, the river of five colours. We're all wearing hats and comfortable clothes and boots, ready to get wet! It's so wonderful here. Hope you're OK.
See you soon,
Aunt Dorothy

A Natalie Roberts
B 17 Green Lane
C York
D YO30 5QX
E UK

Writing Tip

Writing addresses
When we send a postcard, we always write the address of the person we are sending the postcard to. We include the person's **full name**, **house number and street name**, **town/city**, **postcode** and **country** (if we are sending the postcard from another country).

8 a) Look at Natalie's address in Ex. 7. Match the letters (A-E) to the numbers (1-5).

1 ☐ country   4 ☐ town/city
2 ☐ full name   5 ☐ postcode
3 ☐ house number and street name

b) Write the address in the right order.

• UK • EH11 1RP • Alice Denning
• Edinburgh • 9 Napier Drive

Writing Tip

Avoiding repetition
When we write, we use: *it*, *this*, *that*, *here*, *there*, *he*, *she*, etc. to avoid repetition.
*Peter is sitting by the pool. **He** is sunbathing.*
(NOT: ~~Peter is sunbathing.~~)

9 Replace the words in bold with appropriate words to avoid repetition.

Hi Sammy!
My cousin and I are in Croatia for a holiday. **My cousin and I** are staying in a hotel right on the beach. It's quite crowded **on the beach**, but I love it. In the morning, **my cousin and I** go sailing in John's boat. **John's boat** is very fast and we go to the islands near the beach. **The islands near the beach** are very quiet. Seaside restaurants serve local food. **The local food** is delicious!
See you when I get back!
Peter

Writing (a postcard)

10 a) Imagine you are on holiday. Answer the questions.

1 Where are you? ....
2 Who are you with? ....
3 What is the weather like? ....
4 What do you do there every day? ....
5 What are you doing right now? ....
6 What are you wearing? ....
7 Do you like the place? ....

b) Use your ideas from Ex. 10a to write a postcard to your friend Alice (80 words). Use her address from Ex. 8b. Follow the plan.

Plan

Hi + (your friend's first name)
Greetings from … (name of place)
where you are; what the weather is like; what you do there every day; what you are doing right now; what you are wearing; comments/feelings
See you,
(your first name)

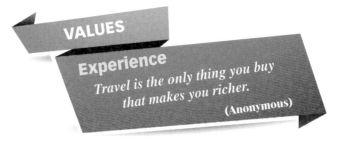

VALUES

Experience
Travel is the only thing you buy that makes you richer.
(Anonymous)

6 Culture

Listening & Reading

 ▶ VIDEO

1 Look at the map. Where is San Francisco; Los Angeles? What is the weather like in these places?

🎧 Listen and read to find out.

OREGON | IDAHO

Redding
Eureka
Lake Tahoe
SACRAMENTO
Napa
Oakland
San Francisco
San Jose
Monterey
Fresno
CALIFORNIA
San Luis Obispo
Bakersfield
PACIFIC OCEAN
Santa Barbara
Los Angeles
Palm Springs
San Diego
ARIZONA
NEVADA
MEXICO

A guide to California

California is around the same **size** as Japan and Morocco. The Sierra Nevada Mountains run down the centre, the Pacific Ocean is to the west and there's a desert in the east.

Read more

State of California	
Nickname: the Golden State	**Capital:** Sacramento
Official language: English	**Largest city:** Los Angeles
Population: about 40 million	**Area:** 423,970 km²

Message board

Hopefultraveller

Hi guys! I'm studying in the US at the moment, and I want to visit California. When's the best time – February? November? April? Where's the best place to go – Los Angeles or San Francisco? And what must I **pack**? Please help!

SanFran01

Come to the City by the Bay – San Francisco! We have dry, sunny weather (15-17°C) from May to October (with some **foggy** days) so you need T-shirts and light clothes. In spring and autumn, it's **wet** but warm. In winter, it's **cool** (the cold months are December and January, with temperatures of around 11°C), so you need some warm clothes like jumpers and trousers, but the important thing is to dress for rain – boots, a hat and a good coat!

LA4ever

La La Land is the place to go! I'm writing this on Redondo Beach in LA in my swimming shorts and it's March! June, July, August and September are all warm – but not too hot (between 20 and 30°C). We have sunny weather all year round, and even in winter it doesn't get very cold (14-15°C). You need a hat for **protection** from the sun, T-shirts, shorts and sandals. A jumper in the winter is just fine.

✓ **Check these words**

desert, pack, protection

2 Read the texts again. Copy and complete the table in your notebook. Then, explain the words in bold.

	San Francisco		Los Angeles	
Season	Winter	Summer	Winter	Summer
Weather	cool		not very cold	
Temperature	11°C	15 – 17°C		20 – 30°C
Must bring			jumper	

Speaking & Writing

3 💭 THINK Use the completed table to compare the climates of Los Angeles and San Francisco.

4 ICT 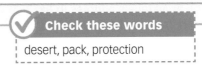 Think of where you live. Create a calendar for your college website showing the weather in each season.

Seasons	Weather	Temperature
winter	cold and snowy	0-5°C

Vocabulary

1 **Fill in:** *foggy, raining, windy, blowing, sunny, freezing.*

1 It's .... cold today.
2 I can't see anything outside. It's ....
3 The wind is ....
4 It's ....; get your umbrella.
5 It's ....; we can fly our kite.
6 It's hot and .... today.

(6 x 2 = 12)

2 **Fill in the clothes.**

1 a girl's shirt = b_ _ _ _ _
2 shoes for the beach = s_ _ _ _ _ _
3 trousers and a jacket for work = s_ _ _
4 a warm top = j_ _ _ _ _
5 shoes for sport = t_ _ _ _ _ _ _
6 a kind of hat = c_ _
7 heavy shoes = b_ _ _ _

(7 x 2 = 14)

Grammar

3 **Write the correct -ing form.**

1 shine – ....
2 run – ....
3 make – ....
4 ski – ....
5 buy – ....
6 have – ....
7 jog – ....
8 visit – ....

(8 X 1 = 8)

4 **Put the verbs in brackets in the present continuous.**

1 We .... **(plan)** to visit Canada this summer.
2 It .... **(not/snow)** now – let's go out and play!
3 .... **(you/play)** on your games console again, Steven?
4 I can't talk now. I .... **(shop)** for sandals with Julie.
5 Martha .... **(enjoy)** her holiday in Spain.
6 William .... **(not/do)** his homework now.

(6 x 3 = 18)

5 **Choose the correct item.**

1 'Is Charlie sleeping?'
  'No, he ....'
  a isn't **b** doesn't
2 'Are you studying?'
  'Yes, I ....'
  a are **b** am
3 'Is it still raining?'
  'No, ...'
  a it isn't **b** isn't it
4 'Are we leaving now?'
  'Yes, ...'
  a we are
  b aren't we
5 'Am I sitting here?'
  'Yes, ...'
  a you are
  b you do

(5 x 2 = 10)

6 **Fill in** *snow, go, have, play, eat, do* **in the** *present continuous* **or** *present simple.*

1 I usually .... jogging in the afternoon, but today I .... to the library.
2 Mark usually .... his homework before dinner, but he .... some jobs for his uncle today.
3 My cousins .... football at the moment, but they usually .... basketball.
4 We .... chicken today, but we usually .... chicken on Saturday.
5 Jill and her family .... dinner in a restaurant now, but they usually .... dinner at home.
6 It .... outside, but it doesn't usually .... in May!

(6 x 3 = 18)

Everyday English

7 **Match the sentences.**

1 ☐ Hello, can I help you?
2 ☐ What size are you?
3 ☐ How about this one?
4 ☐ Have you got it in black?
5 ☐ Can I try it on?

A I'm a medium.
B Sure. The changing rooms are over there.
C I'm looking for a summer dress.
D It looks nice.
E Sure. Here you are.

(5 X 4 = 20)
Total 100

Competences

GOOD ✓

VERY GOOD ✓ ✓

EXCELLENT ✓ ✓ ✓

Lexical Competence
Talk about:
• weather
• seasons
• months
• seasonal activities
• clothes

Reading Competence
• read for specific information (T/F/DS statements; matching; note taking)
Listening Competence
• listen for detail (multiple matching; order pictures)

Speaking Competence
• shop for clothes
Writing Competence
• write a blog post
• write a postcard

Values: Environmentalism

 ► VIDEO

| HOME | ABOUT US | PHOTOS | CONTACT US |

Protect an animal near you!

A lot of animals on our beautiful planet are in danger. Some are very far away – others are right in our own neighbourhood. They all need our help so why not start close to home? Here are five interesting ways to do it!

Put out water

In hot weather, put bowls of water outside your house. Remember, dogs, cats, birds and even hedgehogs get hot and thirsty, too.

Be careful of rubbish!

Animals in towns look for food in rubbish bins. Sometimes they can choke[1] on rubbish or it can poison them. Make sure your rubbish bin has a lid that they can't open!

Grow plants

Find out what local animals eat and plant it in your garden! You can also grow trees to provide food and shelter for garden animals, from insects to birds.

Report strays

Find the number of an animal shelter and tell them when you see stray[2] dogs or cats in the streets. Shelters often run special programmes to help strays.

Drive carefully

In country areas drivers must watch out for animals. They mustn't drive fast so that they don't hit any animals on the road.

[1] choke: stop breathing
[2] stray (animal): without a home

 For more information on how you can help, click here

---

1 Look at the title, the pictures and the headings. **How can we help animals in danger?**
🎧 Listen and read to find out.

2 Read the text again and answer the questions.
  1 Why do we need to put bowls of water outside the house?
  2 How can we make rubbish bins safe for animals?
  3 How can rubbish put local animals' lives in danger?
  4 How do shelters help stray animals?
  5 How can we protect animals on the roads?

3 (THINK) **What is the purpose of the text:** to entertain? to inform? to persuade? **Give reasons.**

4 ICT 💬 **Suggest two more ideas for how to protect animals in your area. Research online for ideas. Use the key words:** ways to help neighbourhood animals. **Use the text in Ex. 1 as a model.**

5 It's Environment Day. Give a talk to members of the club on how to protect animals in your area. You can use your ideas in Ex. 4.

1 **a)** **Read the task.**

> You are an exchange student in London and member of a local environmental organisation. It is World Animal Day. Present an endangered animal to the members of the organisation.

b) 🎧 **Listen to and read the model. Then copy and complete the spidergram in your notebook.**

why endangered • how many left • lives in • lifespan • **endangered animal** • description • weight • eating habits

2 **Which opening technique does Amav use? Replace it with another appropriate one.**

3 **Read the theory. Which closing technique does Amav use? Replace with another technique.**

Closing techniques in public speaking
To end a presentation, we can:
- use a **quote/saying**: In the words of Jack Hanna, *"The most magnificent creature in the entire world, the tiger is."*
- ask a *'what if'* **question**: "What if the red panda disappears? We must make sure that never happens!"
- use a **rhyme** or a **short poem**: As Philo Yan wrote about the lion, *"Magnificent mane of golden brown, He is a king but wears no crown."*

4 **ICT** **Copy the spidergram in Ex. 1b and complete it with information about an endangered animal in your country or another country. Use your notes and the model to prepare and give your presentation.**

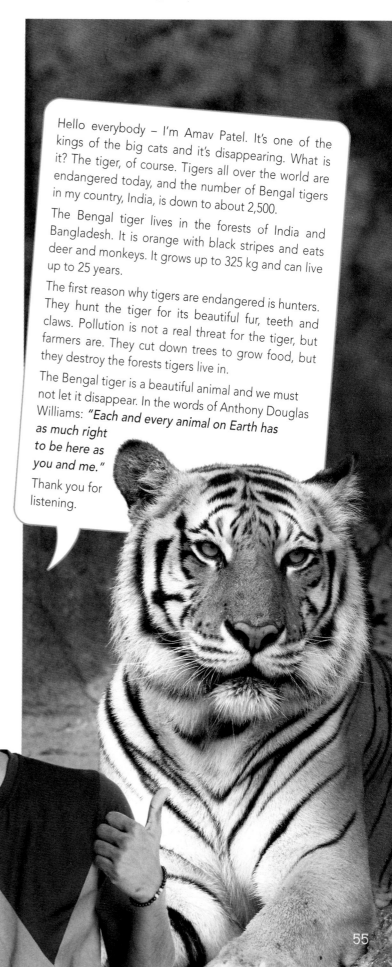

Hello everybody – I'm Amav Patel. It's one of the kings of the big cats and it's disappearing. What is it? The tiger, of course. Tigers all over the world are endangered today, and the number of Bengal tigers in my country, India, is down to about 2,500.

The Bengal tiger lives in the forests of India and Bangladesh. It is orange with black stripes and eats deer and monkeys. It grows up to 325 kg and can live up to 25 years.

The first reason why tigers are endangered is hunters. They hunt the tiger for its beautiful fur, teeth and claws. Pollution is not a real threat for the tiger, but farmers are. They cut down trees to grow food, but they destroy the forests tigers live in.

The Bengal tiger is a beautiful animal and we must not let it disappear. In the words of Anthony Douglas Williams: *"Each and every animal on Earth has as much right to be here as you and me."*

Thank you for listening.

Vocabulary: Types of food/drinks; Cutlery/Tableware; Ways to cook; Food preparation verbs
Grammar: Countable/uncountable nouns; *(How) much/(how) many; A few/a little, Some/any, a lot of;* phrases of quantity; the imperative

Everyday English: Ordering food
Writing: A restaurant review

Taste the world

A pear · strawberries · pineapple · coconut · bananas · grapes · orange · apple · cherries

B coffee · cola · orange juice · tea · water **C** chocolate cake · ice cream · apple pie · pancakes · biscuits

D lettuce · pepper · salad · carrots · onion · garlic · cabbage · potatoes

E cereal · rice · pasta · noodles · bread **F** eggs · cheese · butter · milk

G salt & pepper · mustard & ketchup **H** chicken · lamb · beef **I** fish · crab · prawns

Vocabulary

Food/Drinks

1 Look at the pictures. Match the sections (A-I) to the headings:

vegetables	–	meat & poultry	–	fruit	–
grains	–	sweets	–	drinks	–	dairy & eggs	–
seafood	–	seasoning & sauces

🎧 Listen and check.

2 Answer the questions.

1 Which of the foods/drinks do you like/don't you like?
2 How often do you eat/drink the foods/drinks you like?
3 Which of the foods/drinks above can you have for breakfast/a light meal/dessert?

Speaking

3 🎧 👤👤 Listen to and read the dialogues. Then use the prompts to act out similar dialogues in pairs.

A
A: **I'm thirsty**. Is there anything to drink?
B: **Would you like** some orange juice?
A: No, thanks. I don't like orange juice.
B: **How about** some milk?
A: Oh, yes, please!

B
A: **I'm hungry**. Is there anything to eat?
B: **Would you like** some eggs?
A: No, thanks. I don't like eggs.
B: **How about** some chicken?
A: Oh, yes, please!

- coffee / tea
- cola / water
- pasta / fish
- chicken / noodles

Reading & Listening

4 Look at the pictures (A & B). What are the names of the dishes? What ingredients do we use to make them?

🎧 Listen and read to find out.

▶ VIDEO ⌄ ✕

Food of the World

Are you travelling around the world this year? Local cuisine always adds to your travel experience and helps you to get to know the culture of the country you are visiting better.

A

Ho Chi Minh City, Vietnam

What to eat and drink *Goi Cuon* is a Vietnamese speciality like a spring roll. It has prawns, meat, vegetables and noodles inside rice paper. You dip it in a sweet or salty sauce. Coconut milk is a very refreshing drink to try. The Vietnamese like it a lot.

Culture Tip Most Vietnamese people eat with chopsticks and spoons, but restaurants in Ho Chi Minh City usually have knives and forks too – just ask. Trying chopsticks? Never place them in a V on your plate – it's bad luck!

Did you know? Fish sauce is so popular in Vietnam that there are four different ways to say it in Vietnamese.

B

Tokyo, Japan

What to eat and drink *Okonomiyaki*, or the Japanese pizza, is an excellent choice. *Okonomiyaki* means "what-you-like grill", and in some restaurants you can cook it yourself at your table! It is a pancake they serve with cabbage, meat and nearly any other ingredient you can think of! For a relaxing drink, try matcha latte, milk with green tea powder. You can enjoy it hot or cold.

Culture Tip Don't leave a tip in a Tokyo restaurant. In Japan, they find it strange and a little insulting.

Did you know? The Japanese love seafood. A Japanese person eats 1.2 times their own weight in seafood every year.

 Check these words

cuisine, culture, speciality, salty, sauce, refreshing, chopsticks, ingredient, powder, tip, insulting, weight

---

5 Complete the sentences.

1 Vietnamese spring rolls are a ....
2 A popular drink in Vietnam is ....
3 Vietnamese people usually eat with ....
4 In some Japanese restaurants, you can cook the Japanese pizza ....
5 You can drink milk with green tea powder hot or ....
6 In Japan, it isn't a good idea to ....

6 〈THINK〉 Which dish would you like to try? Why?

Cutlery & Tableware

7 **Fill in:** *knife, fork, plate, bowl, tablespoon, teaspoon.*

1 We can eat soup with a ....

2 We can serve food on a ....

3 We can cut food with a ....

4 We can pick up food with a ....

5 We can eat soup from a ....

6 We can put sugar in tea with a ....

Writing

8 **ICT** Collect information, then write a short text about a typical dish and drink in the capital city of your country for an online travel magazine (60-80 words). Use the subheadings in the text in Ex. 4 to help you.

Grammar in Use

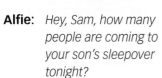

Alfie: Hey, Sam, how many people are coming to your son's sleepover tonight?

Sam: Four. Can you please go to the supermarket for me? I need some ingredients.

Alfie: Sure. What do you need?

Sam: Well, I've got some bananas and an orange, but I haven't got any pears. Can you get me some? And a pineapple, some strawberries and a few peaches.

Alfie: Sure. How many peaches do you need?

Sam: Four are enough. Oh, wait, I need a little yoghurt, too.

Alfie: How much yoghurt do you need?

Sam: One small pot is enough. Oh, and a carton of milk.

Alfie: OK. What are you making with all this fruit anyway?

Sam: Rainbow smoothies!

Alfie: That sounds tasty! Okay, then, off I go!

1 Study the theory. Find examples in the dialogue.

Countable – Uncountable Nouns

- **Countable nouns** are those which we can count. They have singular and plural forms. *1/2/3/4 apple(s)*
- **Uncountable nouns** are those which we cannot count. They have only singular forms.
  some meat/sugar, etc.
- We use *a/an* with countable nouns in the singular.
  a tomato/an egg (NOT: *a sugar*)
- We use *some* with countable nouns in the plural and uncountable nouns in the affirmative.
  *There is **some** bread and **some** biscuits in the cupboard.*
- We use *any* with countable nouns in the plural and uncountable nouns in the negative and interrogative.
  *There aren't **any** apples. Is there **any** milk?*
- We can use *some* for offers or requests.
  *Would you like **some** tea? Can I have **some** pizza?*

2 **a)** Mark the following nouns as Countable *(C)* or Uncountable *(U)*. Then, fill in *a/an* or *some*.

☐ .... honey   ☐ .... tomato   ☐ .... jam

☐ .... burger   ☐ .... coffee   ☐ .... cherry

☐ .... egg   ☐ .... meat   ☐ .... sugar

☐ .... flour   ☐ .... sandwich   ☐ .... butter

☐ .... soup   ☐ .... lemon   ☐ .... peach

b) Write the plurals of the countable nouns in Ex. 2a.

3 Study the theory. Find examples in the dialogue.

Phrases of quantity

We can use countable and uncountable nouns after phrases of quantity such as: *slice, bottle, glass, packet, kilo, loaf, cup, carton, piece + of etc.*

1 a **bottle** of water

2 a **loaf** of bread

3 a **piece** of cheese

4 a **glass** of orange juice

5 a **packet** of pasta

6 a **carton** of milk

7 a **slice** of bread

8 a **cup** of coffee

9 a **bowl** of soup

10 a **bag** of flour

11 a **pot** of yoghurt

12 a **box** of cereal

4 Label the photos. Use: *bread, fruit juice, milk, cereal, cake, olive oil* and the correct phrase of quantity.

1 *two loaves of bread*

2 ....

3 ....

4 ....

5 ....

6 ....

5 Study the theory. Find examples in the dialogue on p. 58.

A lot of/Much/Many – How much/How many – A few/A little

We use *a lot of/lots of* with countable nouns in the affirmative. *There are a lot of/lots of eggs.*
We use *much* with uncountable nouns in the negative and interrogative. *There isn't much coffee. Is there much butter?*
We use *many* with countable nouns in the negative and interrogative. *There aren't many tomatoes. Are there many tomatoes?*
We use *how much* and *a little* (not much but enough) with uncountable nouns.
We use *how many* and *a few* (not many but enough) with countable nouns.
A: *How much milk do you need?*
B: *Just a little.*
A: *How many carrots do you need?*
B: *Just a few.*

6 Choose the correct item.

1 **How much/How many** milk do you need?
2 We need **a little/a few** oranges.
3 There are **much/a lot of** onions in the cupboard.
4 Is there **an/some** egg in the bowl?
5 Would you like **some/any** cake?
6 Is there **many/much** cheese in the fridge?
7 How **much/many** juice do you need? Just **a few/a little**.
8 Are there **some/any** grapes? Yes, there are **a lot/many**.
9 Please buy **a little/a few** cherries.
10 There's too **many/much** salt in the soup.

7 🎧 Tom is making a shopping list for a dinner party. Look at the shopping list, then listen and tick (✓) the things he needs. Finally, ask and answer questions, as in the example.

2 kilos of meat ✓	1 kilo of tomatoes
10 eggs	2 bags of flour
1 kilo of cheese	3 bottles of cola
20 slices of ham	1 carton of orange juice
2 loaves of bread	8 bananas

A: *How much meat does he need?*
B: *He needs two kilos of meat. How many eggs does he need?*
A: *He doesn't need any eggs. ... etc.*

8 SPEAKING 👥 Read the dialogue. Act out similar dialogues. Use the prompts.

A: Would you like some coffee?
B: Yes, please, I'd love some. Would you like some milk?
A: No, thanks. I don't like milk.

• orange juice • chocolate • tea • biscuits • pizza • soda

9 Correct the mistakes.

1 Can I have an banana please?   *a*
2 I'm thirsty. I'd like a water.   ....
3 Can I have any bread, please?   ....
4 I'm hungry. I'd like an burger.   ....
5 Is there many sugar?   ....
6 We haven't got a lot of cake.   ....
7 I'd like some sugars in my tea.   ....
8 How many honey do you need?   ....
9 Could I have a few butter, please?   ....
10 Would you like any milk in your tea?   ....
11 There are much lemons.   ....
12 We need a little potatoes.   ....
13 How many juice is there in the fridge?   ....
14 How much oranges do we need?   ....
15 There's many flour in the cupboard.   ....

10 SPEAKING 👥 THINK You are planning a dinner party for your friends. Decide what you can prepare and write your shopping list.

59

Skills in Action

Vocabulary

Ways to cook

1 a) 🎧 Listen and learn.

bake

boil

roast

fry

grill

b) **How can we cook the foods below?**

- cake • eggs • fish • pasta • chicken
- steak • potatoes

Listening

2 a) **Look at the gaps in the advert. What words do you think are missing? Compare your ideas with your partner's.**

b) 🎧 **Listen and fill in the missing information.**

Name: The [Blue] Lagoon **Type:** Hawaiian

Location: [1] Street

Main Courses: fresh fish dishes, [2] with pineapple.

Desserts: coconut [3]

Cost: £ [4] for two people

Opening hours: 2 pm – [5]

Tel: 6620102

Everyday English

Ordering food

3 **Read the dialogue and fill in the missing words.** 🎧 **Listen and check.**

Waiter:	Good evening, sir. Table **1)** .... two?
Mark:	Yes, please.
Waiter:	This way, please.
Cindy:	Thank you.
Waiter:	Would you like to look **2)** .... the menu?
Cindy:	Thanks.
	_____
Waiter:	May I take your order, please?
Mark:	Yes. I want the tomato soup, to start with.
Cindy:	Tomato soup **3)** .... me, too, please.
Waiter:	Certainly. And for the main course?
Mark:	I'd like the fried fish.
Cindy:	And the grilled chicken for me, please.
Waiter:	Of course. **4)** .... you like something to drink?
Cindy:	A bottle of water, please.
Waiter:	Still or sparkling?
Cindy:	Sparkling, please.
Waiter:	Very well. Would you **5)** .... to order your dessert now?
Mark:	Yes. I'd like the apple pie.
Cindy:	And I'd like a **6)** .... of chocolate cake.
Waiter:	Certainly.

4 **Look at the menu. Act out a dialogue similar to the one in Ex. 3.**

Menu Restaurant

Starters		Desserts	
tomato soup	£4.50	apple pie	£1.80
onion soup	£4.50	fresh fruit	£1.50
grilled vegetables	£4.20	ice-cream	£2.00
Side dishes		carrot cake	£1.80
baked potato	£4.20	**Drinks**	
grilled vegetables	£3.50	Bottled water	£1.00
Main courses		Coffee	£1.20
fried fish	£9.75	Tea	£1.10
grilled chicken	£8.75	Orange juice	£2.20
prawns with rice	£7.75	Hot chocolate	£2.50

Pronunciation /g/, /dʒ/

5 🎧 **Listen and tick (✓). Listen again and repeat.**

	/g/	/dʒ/		/g/	/dʒ/		/g/	/dʒ/
sugar			orange			glass		
ingredient			burger			fridge		

Reading & Writing

6 Read the review, and complete the table.

The Cookhouse

The Cookhouse is the new family restaurant at 10 Bridge Street.

There are a lot of tasty dishes to choose from. For starters, there are fresh salads and spicy soups. The best main courses are pepper steak, roast chicken and fish with rice. Try the Cookhouse's garlic bread – it's delicious. For dessert, have a slice of the chef's superb apple pie or a bowl of the homemade ice cream!

The service is excellent with very helpful and friendly waiters. A meal for two costs about £25 and the restaurant is open from 12 noon to 12 midnight.

The Cookhouse is a great restaurant for any occasion, but it's very busy, so don't forget to book a table first.

Name/Type:	*The Cookhouse/family restaurant*
Location:	
Starters:	
Main courses:	
Sides:	
Desserts:	
Service:	
Cost:	
Opening hours:	
Recommendation:	

7 Complete the gaps with the adjectives in the review in Ex. 6.

1 *new* family restaurant
2 .... dishes
3 .... salads
4 .... soups
5 .... apple pie
6 .... ice cream
7 .... service
8 .... and .... waiters

8 Read the theory. Find examples in the review in Ex. 6.

The imperative

We form the imperative with the base form of the verb. *Book early!*
We form the negative form of the imperative with **Don't + base form of the verb.** *Don't leave a tip.*
We use the imperative to tell people to do or not to do something.

9 Use the verbs in the list in the correct form to complete the sentences.

• forget • try • miss • order • make

1 .... the roast lamb with potatoes. It's delicious.
2 .... out on the prawns with rice.
3 For dessert .... apple pie with ice cream.
4 .... your own pizza or salad.
5 .... to try their traditional dishes, too.

Writing (a restaurant review)

10 **a)** Choose a restaurant you like. Copy the table in Ex. 6 and make notes.

b) Use your notes from Ex. 10a to write a review in English for the restaurant for a local guide for tourists (60-80 words). Follow the plan. Mind the punctuation.

Plan

Para 1: name of the restaurant, type, location
Para 2: starters, main courses, desserts
Para 3: service, cost, opening hours
Para 4: recommendation

Writing Tip

Using adjectives
Use a variety of adjectives to make your writing more interesting.
*The service is **good**. The service is **excellent**!*

VALUES

Health
Eat to live, not live to eat.
(proverb)

7 Culture

◄ ► RECIPES | LIFESTYLE AND EVENTS | NEW! FAMILY & KIDS | MORE GOOD FOOD |

Traditional Recipes > Ireland

Ireland, the Emerald Isle, is famous for its cuisine.
Do you want to learn how to cook traditional Irish dishes yourself?
Then we have everything you need. Why not send in your own recipes for others to try?

 From Kathleen:

Boxty (Irish potato pancakes)

Ingredients:
4 large potatoes
1 egg
100 g flour
150 ml milk
baking powder
salt

Instructions:
Peel and grate the potatoes into small pieces and put them into a towel.
Squeeze all the juice out of the potatoes.
Mix the flour, salt and baking powder together.
Beat the egg.
Mix the flour, salt and baking powder with the egg and potatoes.
Use a tablespoon to get part of the mixture and put it in a hot frying pan.
Fry until cooked on both sides. Repeat with the rest of the mixture.
Perfect for breakfast!

Follow us

 From Patrick:

Irish stew

Ingredients:
lamb (a kilo)
6 potatoes
4 onions
4 carrots
water
salt and pepper

Instructions:
Cut the lamb into large pieces and season with salt and pepper.
Fry lamb pieces in a large pot until they are brown.
Put meat aside, then cut the onions, carrots and potatoes into large pieces, and cook in the pot until brown.
Put the meat into the pot and add water.
Cook for an hour.

 Check these words

recipe, baking powder, instructions, towel, frying pan, season, pot

Vocabulary
Food preparation

1 🎧 **Listen and learn.**

peel

grate

beat

mix

add

cut

Listening & Reading

2 **Look at the dishes on the webpage. Which country are they from? Which contains:** *onions? an egg?*
🎧 **Listen and read to find out.**

Speaking & Writing

3 👥 **Choose one of the dishes. Ask and answer questions about what ingredients you need and how to make it.**

4 **ICT Think of a traditional dish in your country. Write the recipe for an international online cooking magazine. Use photos. You can cook the dish and record a video of yourselves to show the class.**

Vocabulary

1 **Circle the odd one out.**

1 coconut – pineapple – apple pie – pear
2 carrot – orange – onion – potato
3 cake – ice cream – biscuit – cheese
4 pepper – fish – prawn – crab
5 milk – soup – tea – juice
6 salt – cereal – rice – pasta

(6 x 2 = 12)

2 **Label the items in the picture.**

1 g.....................
6 b.....................
2 k.....................
5 f.....................
3 t.....................
4 p.....................

(6 x 2 = 12)

3 **Fill in:** *roast, peel, boil, beat, bake, squeeze, add, fry.*

1 .... the pasta in water with salt in it.
2 We .... a cake every Sunday.
3 .... two oranges to get the juice.
4 .... the fish in olive oil.
5 .... five potatoes and cut them into pieces.
6 .... pepper to make your soup spicy.
7 .... your chicken for 2 hours at 220°C.
8 .... three eggs with a little milk and some flour.

(8 x 2 = 16)

4 **Complete the words.**

1 You serve soup in a b _ _ _ .
2 You need a r _ _ _ _ _ to make a dish.
3 The w _ _ _ _ _ _ in the restaurant are very helpful.
4 Cereal and rice are g _ _ _ _ _ .
5 Prawns and crab are s _ _ _ _ _ _ .
6 What i _ _ _ _ _ _ _ _ _ _ do we need to make Irish stew?
7 Apple pie and ice cream are d _ _ _ _ _ _ _ .

(7 x 2 = 14)

Grammar

5 **Write *C* for Countable or *U* for Uncountable.**

1 jam ....   6 chip ....
2 egg ....   7 coffee ....
3 rice ....   8 soup ....
4 oil ....   9 grape ....
5 banana ....   10 cherry ....

(10 x 1 = 10)

6 **Choose the correct item.**

1 a **loaf/carton** of bread
2 a **bottle/packet** of oil
3 a **bowl/slice** of cereal
4 a **bag/pot** of yoghurt
5 a **slice/glass** of cake
6 a **cup/carton** of tea
7 a **piece/bowl** of cheese
8 a **pot/glass** of juice
9 a **loaf/packet** of pasta
10 a **carton/piece** of milk

(10 x 1 = 10)

7 **Fill in** *much, many, little, few, some (x2), any (x2).*

1 There aren't .... tomatoes for the salad.
2 Do we have .... food in the fridge?
3 Sam is drinking .... water.
4 There's a .... ice cream – do you want it?
5 Can I have .... sugar in my tea?
6 How .... cups are on the table?
7 There are only a .... eggs in the box – I need more.
8 How .... sauce do you want?

(8 x 2 = 16)

Everyday English

8 **Match the sentences.**

1 ☐ Would you like something to drink?
2 ☐ Can I take your order?
3 ☐ How's your pizza?
4 ☐ We'd like a table for three.
5 ☐ Can we have the bill, please?

A This way, please.
B Of course, madam.
C For a starter, I want a salad.
D A bottle of water, please.
E Delicious. How about yours?

(5 x 2 = 10)

Total 100

Competences

GOOD ✓
VERY GOOD ✓✓
EXCELLENT ✓✓✓

Lexical Competence
Talk about:
• types of food/drinks
• tableware/cutlery
• meals
• ways to cook
• food preparation verbs

Reading Competence
• read for specific information (sentence completion; note taking)
Listening Competence
• listen for specific information (gap-fill)

Speaking Competence
• make a shopping list
• order food at a restaurant
Writing Competence
• write a text about a dish in my country • write a restaurant review • write a recipe

Vocabulary: Adjectives describing places, tourist attractions
Grammar: comparative/superlative, adverbs of degree; *too/enough*

Everyday English: making suggestions
Writing: An article about a place

New places, new faces

Vocabulary
Adjectives describing places

1 Use the adjective-noun collocations to make sentences about York and Los Angeles, as in the example.

York, UK

Los Angeles, USA

York is a quiet place, while LA is a noisy place.
York has got clean streets ...

quiet ≠ noisy	place
clean ≠ dirty/polluted	streets
tall ≠ small	buildings/houses
cheap ≠ expensive	shops/hotels/restaurants
modern ≠ old	city/town
exciting ≠ boring	nightlife

2 Look at the pictures in Ex. 1 and use the adjectives below to compare the two places, as in the examples.

- noisier • more expensive • cleaner • quieter
- more modern • more polluted • cheaper • older
- more crowded

*LA is **noisier than** York.*
*LA is **more expensive than** York.*

Reading

3 🗣🗣 Read the text quickly. Which of these sentences are *T* (true) about Los Angeles? Decide in pairs.

🎧 Listen, read and check.

1 All the hotels in LA are very expensive. ....
2 Venice Beach is famous for its Botanical Gardens. ....
3 Melrose Avenue is famous for its expensive shops. ....
4 A lot of restaurants in LA are open 24 hours. ....
5 The Hollywood Bowl is an outdoor theatre. ....

4 Read the text again and answer the questions.

1 Where can you stay in LA? Which places are special? Why?
2 Where can you see handprints of famous actors?
3 Where can you find modern cheap clothes?
4 What can you do at the Grand Central Market?
5 What can you do at the Staples Center?

5 Choose words from the list to fill in the gaps. Then use them to make sentences based on the text.

- film • heavy • sunny • designer • sports
- expensive • street • outdoor

1	.... stars	5	.... clothes
2	.... weather	6	.... shops
3	.... traffic	7	.... theatre
4	.... performers	8	.... stadium

6 Match the words in bold in the text to their synonyms in the list. You can use your dictionary.

- trendy • delicious • memorable
- interesting • bright • near

64

▶ VIDEO

Los Angeles
THE CITY OF ANGELS

Los Angeles is the second largest city in America. It's also home to museums, film stars, **sunny** weather, tall buildings and heavy traffic along with 75 miles of coastline.

ACCOMMODATION

Hotels in LA can be more expensive than those in many other American cities, but there are much cheaper ones as well to suit everyone's budget. Choose one **close to** special bus stops where you can get rides to the city sights.

PLACES TO VISIT

Don't miss Venice Beach with its street performers, Universal Studios to see how they make films, and Griffith Park with its Botanical Gardens. You can also see the handprints and footprints of film stars outside Grauman's Chinese Theatre. Children can visit the Children's Museum – one of the most exciting museums in the world.

SHOPPING

You can buy very **fashionable** clothes on Melrose Avenue and they're quite cheap. For designer clothes, go to the expensive shops on Rodeo Drive. A visit there is always **unforgettable**.

EATING OUT

LA has a lot of restaurants to eat at, serving Asian, Italian, Mexican food and more! Many of them are 24-hour restaurants. And don't forget to visit Grand Central Market – it's got 37 stalls offering **tasty** dishes from all over the world.

ENTERTAINMENT

The Hollywood Bowl is bigger than any other outdoor theatre in America. You can watch a concert under the stars. Or spend the evening at the Staples Center and watch a basketball match in the huge sports stadium. There's nowhere better!

LA is one of the most popular cities with visitors in the USA. It's noisy and crowded, but it's also **fascinating**.

✓ **Check these words**

home to, star, along with, suit everyone's budget, stall

Speaking

7 Tell the class three reasons why LA is an ideal city for a holiday. Find someone in the class that shares the same reasons as you.

Writing

8 THINK Write sentences comparing your city/town/village to LA.

Mexico City is crowded and noisy.
LA is crowded and noisy, too.

Grammar in Use

Visit the Big Apple!

They call New York City 'the Big Apple' because it's big in every way. In fact it's home to the tallest building in the USA – the One World Trade Center. It's also the biggest city in the USA – over 8.5 million people live there. It has a larger number of people from foreign countries than any other city in the world. New York is more popular with tourists than any other US destination, with about 60 million visitors every year. With all those people, it is one of the busiest places in the world. New York is the most exciting city you can visit. There's nowhere better than 'the Big Apple' for people looking for something memorable!

Five nights £685 – flights included!

1 Read the theory. How do we form the comparative/superlative forms of adjectives? Find examples in the advert.

Comparative – Superlative

	adjective	comparative	superlative
one-syllable adjectives	cheap large big	cheaper (than) larger (than) bigger (than)	the cheapest the largest the biggest
-y adjectives	noisy	noisier	the noisiest
adjectives with two or more syllables	expensive	more expensive	the most expensive
irregular adjectives	good bad much many little	better worse more less	the best the worst the most the least

- We use the **comparative form** to compare two people, things, places, etc. We usually use **than** with comparative adjectives.
  *Birmingham is **bigger than** Edinburgh but it is **smaller than** London.*
- We use the **superlative form** to compare more than two people, things, places. We use **the ... of** with superlative adjectives.
  *London is **the biggest of** all. Edinburgh is **the smallest of** all.*

2 Use the forms in the advert to complete the table.

adjective	comparative	superlative
tall	taller	
big	bigger	
large		the largest
popular		the most popular
busy	busier	
exciting	more exciting	
good		the best

3 Put the adjectives in brackets into the comparative.

1 Los Angeles is .... (**hot**) than New York.
2 Some people think New York is .... (**fashionable**) than Los Angeles.
3 The weather is .... (**bad**) in New York than in Los Angeles.
4 It's .... (**cheap**) to fly from London to New York than Los Angeles.
5 You can get a .... (**tasty**) taco in New York than in Los Angeles.
6 The beaches in Los Angeles are .... (**nice**) than the ones in New York.

4 Put the adjectives in the correct form to fill in the gaps. Add any necessary words.

1 Bangkok is .... (**large**) Astana but Melbourne is .... (**large**) of all.
2 Melbourne is .... (**warm**) Astana but Bangkok is .... (**warm**) of all.
3 Melbourne is .... (**noisy**) Astana but Bangkok is .... (**noisy**) of all.
4 Bangkok is .... (**expensive**) Astana but Melbourne is .... (**expensive**) of all.

5 SPEAKING In pairs, use the adjectives below to compare cities in your country.

- cold • small • quiet • cheap • large • sunny

A: .... *is colder than ... .*
B: .... *is the coldest city in my country.*

6 Fill in the superlative forms and choose the correct answer (A, B or C).

🎧 Listen and check your answers.

1 Which is .... **(large)** desert in the world?
   A the Sahara   **B** the Namib   **C** the Nevada

2 Which is .... **(high)** mountain in the world?
   A Ben Nevis   **C** Mount Everest
   B Mount McKinley

3 Which is .... **(long)** river in the world?
   A the Missouri   **C** the Amazon
   B the Mississippi

4 Where is .... **(dry)** place in the world?
   A in Chile   **B** in Canada   **C** in Australia

5 Which is .... **(small)** country in the world?
   A Luxembourg   **C** the State of Vatican City
   B Wales

6 Where is .... **(tall)** building in the USA?
   A Dallas   **B** New York   **C** Chicago

7 Read the theory. Make sentences, as in the examples.

Comparative - Adverbs of degree

- We can use **(not) as + adjective + as** to compare two places, things, people etc.
  *York isn't **as noisy as** Los Angeles.*
- **much + comparative**.
  *York is **much quieter than** LA.*
- **quite/very** + adjective.
  *York is **quite expensive** but LA is **very expensive**.*
- **too** + adjective (negative meaning).
  *LA is **too noisy**. I can't stand the noise.*
- **adjective + enough** (positive meaning)
  *Tickets to York are **cheap enough**.*

	buses	trains	taxis
expensive	✓	✓✓	✓✓✓
safe	✓✓	✓✓✓	✓
fast	✓	✓✓✓	✓✓
comfortable	✓	✓✓✓	✓✓

*Buses in Britain aren't **as expensive as** trains.*
*Taxis in Britain are **much more expensive** than buses.*
*Trains in Britain are **very expensive**.*
*Taxis in Britain are **too expensive**.*
*Buses in Britain are **cheap enough**.*

8 🎧 Read the sentences, then listen and decide if they are *T* (true) or *F* (false). Make sentences, as in the examples.

London
Edinburgh

1 Edinburgh is smaller than London.   *T*
   That's true. London isn't as small as Edinburgh.
   Edinburgh is much smaller than London.

2 London is safer than Edinburgh.   *F*
   That's false. London isn't as safe as Edinburgh.
   Edinburgh is much safer than London.

3 Edinburgh is noisier than London.   ....

4 London is more polluted than Edinburgh.   ....

5 London is cheaper than Edinburgh.   ....

9 a) Use the key language to fill in the gaps.

- quite (✓) • very (✓✓) • much (✓✓✓) • too (✗)

A: Shall we go to Mykonos for our summer holidays?
B: Well, it looks **1)** .... (✓✓) nice but I think it's **2)** .... (✗) expensive for us.
A: Why don't we go to Santorini then? It's **3)** .... (✓✓✓) cheaper than Mykonos and **4)** .... (✓) easy to get to.
B: OK, let's go there then.

b) Use the prompts to act out similar dialogues.

Johannesburg
exciting (✓✓), crowded (✗)
San Jose
interesting (✓✓), noisy (✗)

Cape Town
beautiful (✓✓✓), quiet (✓)
Drake Bay
pretty (✓✓✓), peaceful (✓)

10 SPEAKING 👥 Discuss your city/town using the prompts below, as in the example.

- old building • large park • busy road/street
- popular café • expensive restaurant
- famous square • pretty building

A: Which is the oldest building in ...?
B: I think the Town Hall is the oldest building in my city. Which is the largest park?

67

Skills in Action

Vocabulary
Tourist attractions

1 **a)** **What can you do in each of these places? Choose from the list and make sentences.**

- watch a performance • see paintings
- buy souvenirs • go for a walk • try local dishes
- go on rides • watch a football match • see statues

restaurant

museum

art gallery

sports stadium

theme park

theatre

gift shop

park

We can see paintings in an art gallery.

b) **Which of these places are there in your city?**

Listening

2 🎧 **Listen to the dialogue and match the people (1-5) to the places (A-G). There is an example. There is one extra place.**

People		Places	
0	D Liam	**A**	sports stadium
1	☐ Sally	**B**	restaurant
2	☐ Ralph	**C**	museum
3	☐ Helen	**D**	art gallery
4	☐ Ronny	**E**	theme park
5	☐ Mary	**F**	market
		G	theatre

Everyday English
Making suggestions

3 **Sam and Lee are trying to decide where to go on their first day in LA. What do they decide to do?**

🎧 **Listen and read to find out.**

Sam	Morning, Lee. The hotel's lovely, isn't it?
Lee:	Hi, Sam! Yes, it's very comfortable. Now, what's the plan for our first day in LA?
Sam:	I know – let's go shopping! LA has great gift shops! We can buy souvenirs to bring home.
Lee:	I don't really feel like shopping on the first day of our trip. How about going to a museum – like the Getty Centre?
Sam:	Well, I don't really like museums. How about visiting the Universal Studios theme park?
Lee:	OK, that sounds like fun. And after that we can go to a restaurant and try some local dishes.
Sam:	Sure, let's do that.

4 👥 **Imagine you are in LA. Use phrases from the Useful Language box and the places below to act out a dialogue like the one in Ex. 3.**

- the Los Angeles Theatre • the LA Galaxy stadium
- The Aquarium of the Pacific • Grand Park

Making suggestions	
• Let's/Why don't we/Shall we (go/visit, etc)	
• How/What about (going/visiting, etc)	
• Do you fancy/What do you say to (going/visiting, etc)	
Accepting suggestions	**Refusing suggestions**
• What a good idea!	• I don't really feel like ... .
• Sure, why not.	• No, let's not do that.
• That sounds great!	• That doesn't sound like fun!
• I'd love to.	• I'd rather not.

Pronunciation /s/ /ʃ/

5 🎧 **Listen and tick (✓). Listen again and repeat.**

	/s/	/ʃ/		/s/	/ʃ/
shopping			shall		
sunbathing			fashionable		
sightseeing			sunny		

Reading & Writing

6 Read the task. Look at the underlined key words and complete the sentences.

A <u>travel website</u> wants its readers to write an <u>article about a popular tourist destination in their country</u>. Write your article for the website <u>describing what visitors can see and do there</u> (80-120 words).

1 I need to write an .... about .... describing ....
2 It is for a ....
3 I need to write .... words.

7 a) Read the article. Copy and complete the spidergram in your notebook.

Stratford-upon-Avon

In the UK? Not sure where to go?
Then pay a visit to Stratford-upon-Avon, just north-west of London.

This pretty, historic town is full of peaceful parks and the wide River Avon runs through it. There's so much to do! You can eat at one of the local restaurants next to the river or go for a walk to see the traditional houses. Of course, Stratford is famous because it is the birthplace of William Shakespeare. You can visit his old home or watch one of his popular plays at the Royal Shakespeare Theatre.

It's a must-see for visitors to the UK and it's only two hours by train from London. So what are you waiting for?
Head for Stratford!

b) THINK What is the author's purpose?

8 Find the adjectives in the text in Ex. 7 that describe: *town, parks, River Avon, restaurants, houses, home, plays*.

9 Circle the odd adjective out.

1 historic – pretty – sandy – old **town**
2 quiet – delicious – busy – trendy **streets**
3 traditional – warm – modern – large **houses**
4 fine – local – outdoor – long **restaurants**

Writing (an article about a place)

Writing Tip

Articles describing a popular tourist destination can appear in magazines, on blogs, etc. They normally consist of:
• an **introduction** in which we give general information about the place (name, location, etc.).
• a **main body** in which we write what we can see and do there.
• a **conclusion** in which we write our comments and/or feelings about the place.
We always give our article a **short catchy** title to attract the reader's attention. We normally use **present tenses** and **informal language** (short verb forms; simple linkers; everyday language). We can use **adjectives** to make our description more interesting to the reader.

10 a) **ICT** Copy the spidergram in Ex. 7 into your notebook. Collect information about a popular tourist destination in your country and complete the spidergram.

b) Use your notes in Ex. 10a to write your article for the website. Follow the plan. You can use the article in Ex. 7 as a model.

Plan

Title (name of city/town/village)
Introduction: name & location of city/town/village
Main body: what to see and do there
Conclusion: comments/recommendation

VALUES

Adventure
Wherever you go, go with all your heart.
(Confucius)

▶ VIDEO

◁ | ▷ HOME | ABOUT US | SPECIAL OFFERS! | DESTINATIONS | CONTACT   🔍

Welcome to New Zealand

Welcome to New Zealand, the country of 'The Lord of the Rings'. This beautiful country is full of surprises for all travellers. From the tallest mountains in Oceania to the huge volcanoes, there are so many places to visit!

A

B

C

D

Places to visit:

Milford Sound is one of the most beautiful places on Earth. Up to a million people visit this fjord on New Zealand's South Island every year. The clear water, beautiful waterfalls and fantastic views are a must-see for every visitor to New Zealand.

Things to do: Trekking, kayaking and boat cruises.

Tongariro National Park is New Zealand's oldest national park. It's like no other place in the world. Inside the park is New Zealand's highest volcano, as well as lakes and waterfalls.

Things to do: Camping, skiing and mountain biking.

New adventures are waiting for you!

Click <u>here</u> to find out more.

FUN FACT:

New Zealand's name in Maori is Aotearoa, the land of the long white cloud.

✓ **Check these words**

must-see, trekking

Listening & Reading

1 Which photo (A-D) shows: *a volcano*? *a waterfall*? *a lake*? *a fjord*? **Which of these can you see in Tongariro National Park?**

🎧 **Listen and read to find out.**

2 Read again and answer the questions.

1 How many people visit Milford Sound every year?
2 What can visitors to Milford Sound see?
3 What can visitors to Tongariro National Park do?
4 What does New Zealand's name in Maori mean?

Speaking & Writing

3 (THINK) 👥 **Put the places in the text in order of interest. Which one would you like to visit? Why?**

4 **ICT** **Collect information about two places of natural beauty in your country or in another country. What geographical features make each special? What can visitors do there? Write short texts. Alternatively, prepare a digital presentation. Use photos.**

Vocabulary

1 **Fill in:** *traffic, buildings, clothes, weather, shops.*

Milan in northern Italy is one of the world's biggest fashion capitals. It's full of expensive **1)** .... and is the ideal place to buy designer **2)** .... You can see lots of interesting sights there and enjoy the sunny **3)** .... in the summer. Milan is an old city and it doesn't have many tall **4)** .... It has a lot of heavy **5)** .... though, so it's better to use public transport to get around.

(5 x 2 = 10)

2 **Choose the correct adjective.**

1 Megan always wears **fashionable/tasty** clothes.
2 Paris is a **fascinating/bright** place to visit.
3 Italian ice cream is really **trendy/delicious**.
4 Our hotel is **quiet/noisy** because it's in the city centre.
5 The streets in LA are very **crowded/heavy**.

(5 x 2 = 10)

3 **Fill in:** *park, gallery, stadium, shop.*

1 art .... 3 gift ....
2 sports .... 4 theme ....

(4 x 2 = 8)

4 **Fill in:** *go (x2), see, watch (x2), buy.*

1 .... on rides 4 .... souvenirs
2 .... a football match 5 .... a performance
3 .... for a walk 6 .... statues

(6 x 2 = 12)

Grammar

5 **Choose the correct item.**

1 Florence is **most/more** beautiful than Rome.
2 This is the **luxurious/most luxurious** hotel of all.
3 This restaurant is **cheaper/cheapest** than that one.
4 Which is the **noisier/noisiest** city in the USA?
5 What is the **better/best** way to travel?

(5 x 2 = 10)

6 **Complete the sentences with the correct form of the adjectives in brackets.**

1 This is .... (expensive) restaurant in town.
2 The Sahara Desert is one of .... (hot) places on Earth.
3 This museum is not .... (interesting) as the art gallery.
4 The Eiffel Tower is .... (tall) than the Statue of Liberty.
5 The market is .... (crowded) on Saturdays than on Fridays.

(5 x 4 = 20)

7 **Choose the correct item.**

A: This hotel looks **1) very/too** nice.
B: Yes, and it's not **2) much/too** expensive.
A: But it's in the city centre. I think it's **3) too/much** noisy for us.
B: OK, how about this one? It looks **4) quite/much** quieter.
A: Yes, and it's **5) quite/too** close to the airport.

(5 x 2 = 10)

Everyday English

8 **Match the exchanges.**

1 ☐ The hotel's lovely.
2 ☐ What's the plan for today?
3 ☐ How about going to the museum?
4 ☐ Why don't we go to the sports stadium?
5 ☐ We can go to the art gallery.

A Well, I don't really like museums.
B OK. Let's do that.
C Yes, it's very comfortable.
D I know – let's go shopping.
E I'd rather not. I don't like football.

(5 x 4 = 20)

Total 100

Competences

GOOD ✓
VERY GOOD ✓✓
EXCELLENT ✓✓✓

Lexical Competence
Talk about
• places in a city
• tourist attractions

Reading Competence
• read for specific information (T/F statements; answer questions)
• read for gist (identify author's purpose)

Listening Competence
• listen for specific information (multiple matching)

Speaking Competence
• make suggestions – accept/refuse suggestions

Writing Competence
• write sentences comparing your town/city to LA
• write an article describing a place

71

9

Vocabulary: Features in a place, Places/Buildings in a town/city, Transport
Grammar: past simple *(was/were, had, could)*
Everyday English: Asking for/Giving directions
Writing: An article about your neighbourhood

Times change

Vocabulary

Features in a place

1 **Look at the pictures. Which shows:**

1 fishing boats ☐
2 a souvenir shop ☐
3 a stone cottage ☐
4 a ferry boat ☐
5 an airport ☐
6 a guest house ☐

2 🎧 **Read the summary. There are four mistakes in it. Guess which they are. Listen to and read the main text to check.**

Inishmore is a beautiful island off the east coast of Ireland. Seventy years ago, life was difficult there. People only had bicycles and small fishing boats to move around. Their houses didn't have electricity, but they had running water. Nowadays, there is an airport and big ferry boats. Visitors can stay in hotels and try local dishes in restaurants. There aren't any green fields now, but people are happy.

Inishmore: Then & Now

Inishmore is a beautiful little island off the west coast of Ireland. At first, Inishmore seems **exactly** the same as it was seventy years ago, but **in fact** it is a very different place today.

Colman Coneely, a 90-year-old islander, says, "When I was young, tourists couldn't **reach** Inishmore. There wasn't an airport or any ferry boats in those days. There were only donkeys and small fishing boats for **getting around**. Life was difficult. We didn't have much money — we only had small stone cottages. We didn't even have **electricity** or running water! Inishmore was a quiet place — there weren't any guest houses or restaurants **back then**."

✓ **Check these words**

coast, seem, islander, get around

Today, up to 2,000 tourists a day can visit Inishmore. "Now there is an airport," says Colman. "There are also cars, buses, bicycles and big ferry boats. Life is very easy now. We have got new, modern houses and a lot of money. We have also got electricity and running water. Inishmore is very busy now. There are guest houses, restaurants and lots of souvenir shops."

Colman looks across the green fields in front of his house and smiles. "One thing is the same. Inishmore is still beautiful and we're **working hard** to keep it just like this."

Reading

3 **a)** **Read the article and answer the questions.**

1 Where is Inishmore?
2 Why couldn't tourists reach the island seventy years ago?
3 How did the islanders get around?
4 How can tourists reach Inishmore today?
5 What does Colman Coneely think of the island?

b) (THINK) **Give the article another title.**

4 **Choose words from the list to fill in the gaps, then use them to make sentences based on the text.**

• water • fields • cottages • houses • shops • boats

1 fishing ....
2 stone ....
3 running ....

4 guest ....
5 souvenir ....
6 green........................

5 **Write the opposites of the adjectives in bold. Use the words in the list. Then, make sentences using the phrases.**

• busy • easy • big • same

1 a **little** island ≠ a .... island
2 a **different** place ≠ the .... place
3 a **quiet** place ≠ a .... place
4 **difficult** life ≠ .... life

6 **Explain the words/phrases in bold. You can use your dictionary.**

Speaking & Writing

7 **Look at the table and make notes under the headings in your notebook.**

THEN	NOW
what there was/wasn't & what people had/didn't have	what there is & what people have got

Now, look at your notes and talk about what Inishmore was like seventy years ago and what it is like now. Start like this:

There wasn't an airport on Inishmore then. There were only donkeys and fishing boats ...

8 (THINK) **How is the place where you live the same as/different to Inishmore? Write a few sentences. Read them to the class.**

Grammar in Use

1 **Do the quiz.**

🎧 **Listen and check.**

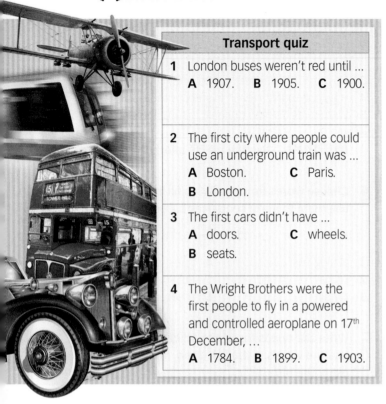

Transport quiz
1 London buses weren't red until ... **A** 1907.   **B** 1905.   **C** 1900.
2 The first city where people could use an underground train was ... **A** Boston.   **C** Paris. **B** London.
3 The first cars didn't have ... **A** doors.   **C** wheels. **B** seats.
4 The Wright Brothers were the first people to fly in a powered and controlled aeroplane on 17th December, ... **A** 1784.   **B** 1899.   **C** 1903.

2 **Read the table. Find two examples in the quiz.**

was/were (past simple of the verb *to be*)	
Affirmative	**Negative**
I/he/she/it **was** you/we/they **were**	I/he/she/it **was not/wasn't** you/we/they **were not/weren't**
Interrogative	**Short answers**
Was I/he/she/it ...? **Were** you/we/they ...?	Yes, I/he/she/it **was**. No, I/he/she/it **wasn't**. Yes, you/we/they **were**. No, you/we/they **weren't**.

Time expressions: last week/month etc, a week/two days ago etc, yesterday afternoon/evening etc.

3 **Fill in:** *was*, *were*, *wasn't* **or** *weren't*.

1 The Maya civilisation .... an important one in Central America from 2000 BCE to 1700 CE.
2 Some Maya people .... rich, but most ....; they .... very poor, and .... farmers or slaves.
3 Their favourite drink .... chocolate but it .... cheap so it .... only for the rich.
4 The 17th century .... the end of the Maya civilisation.

4 **a)** **Fill in** *were*, *was* **or** *wasn't*.

A: **1)** .... you at home last night?
B: No, I **2)** .... I **3)** .... **at the cinema.**
A: Who **4)** .... you with?
B: I **5)** .... with **Claire.**
A: How **6)** .... **the film**?
B: It **7)** .... **very good**. It **8)** .... **boring** at all. Where **9)** .... you?
A: I **10)** .... at home.
B: **11)** .... you with **Sally**?
A: No, I **12)** .... **She 13)** .... **at work**.

b) 🗣️🗣️ **Use the prompts to act out a dialogue like the one in Ex. 4a.**

• at a restaurant • Sharon • the food • not very nice • horrible • Craig • at a football match

5 🗣️🗣️ **Use the prompts below to ask and answer questions about London 150 years ago, as in the example.**

• hotels (✓) • post offices (✓) • blocks of flats (✗)
• horses (✓) • electricity (✗) • phone boxes (✗)
• tea rooms (✓) • an airport (✗) • theatres (✓)
• a football stadium (✗)

A: *Were there any hotels in London 150 years ago?*
B: *Yes, there were. Were there any ...?*

6 **Read the table. Find an example in the quiz in Ex. 1.**

Had (past simple of *have*)	
Affirmative	I/you/he, etc **had**
Negative	I/you/he, etc **didn't have**
Interrogative	**Did** I/you/he, etc. **have**
Short answers	Yes, I/you/he, etc. **did**. No, I/you/he, etc. **didn't**.

7 **Fill in:** *have*, *had* **or** *didn't have*.

1 In the 1950s, people .... black and white TVs. Nowadays, people .... flat screen TV sets.
2 Nowadays, we .... electronic books, but not very long ago we only .... paper books.
3 Before the 20th century, people .... planes to travel far away. They only .... ships. These days, we .... ships and planes.
4 Early cars .... steering wheels. Now, all of them .... steering wheels.

74

8 **a)** **Look at the pictures. Tick (✓) what people had 100 years ago. Then, in pairs, ask and answer questions, as in the example.**

helicopters 1939 ☐   hot-air balloons 1783 ☐   mobile phones 1973 ☐

GPS devices 1989 ☐   typewriters 1867 ☐   computers 1939 ☐

telephones 1876 ☐   cars 1886 ☐   USB flash drives 1999 ☐

A: *Did they have helicopters?*
B: *No, they didn't. Did they have ...*

b) **Now write sentences, as in the example.**

People didn't have helicopters 100 years ago.

9 **Read the table. Find an example in the quiz in Ex. 1.**

Could (past simple of *can*)	
Affirmative	I/you/he, etc **could** swim.
Negative	I/you/he, etc **couldn't** swim.
Interrogative	**Could** I/you/he, etc swim?
Short answers	Yes, I/you/he, etc **could**. No, I/you/he, etc **couldn't**.

10 **a)** 🎧 **Listen to the two men talking about themselves and fill in the missing ages. Then make sentences, as in the example.**

Paul could talk when he was one, but Doug couldn't talk until he was two.

	Paul	Doug
talk	1	2
count	....	3
read	2	5
walk	2	....
ride a bicycle	....	10
swim	....	....

b) **Now talk about yourself, as in the example.**

I could talk when I was one, but I couldn't count until I was three. ...

11 **Fill in** *were(n't)*, *had*, *didn't have*, *was* **or** *could(n't)*.

Some ancient Romans **1)** .... very rich and they **2)** .... beautiful brick houses. However, there **3)** .... any windows on the outside walls and there **4)** .... any carpets on the floors! Other people **5)** .... smaller houses or flats. Ancient Rome **6)** .... big streets – the streets were narrow. There **7)** .... lots of theatres and in every town and city there **8)** .... a market and public baths. The public baths **9)** .... very popular. Men and women **10)** .... go there at different times, but children **11)** .... use the baths. Hunting, riding, fishing and having dinner parties with friends **12)** .... also popular free-time activities. There **13)** .... lots of games and toys for children. The boys' favourite games **14)** .... ball games and the girls **15)** .... dolls to play with. Children also **16)** .... dogs, cats, ducks and geese as pets. The ancient Romans' favourite food **17)** .... meat. Rich Romans **18)** .... big feasts with lots of meat, but the poor **19)** .... afford it, so they **20)** .... vegetables and porridge.

12 **a)** LISTENING **Do the quiz about ancient Inca children.**

🎧 **Listen and check.**

1 Ancient Inca children had ...
  A paper books.   **B** wooden toys.
2 They could ...
  A cook, farm and fish.   **B** read and write.
3 Their favourite food was ...
  A potatoes and corn.   **B** meat with quinoa.
4 Their favourite games were ...
  A ball games.   **B** board games.

b) SPEAKING **Compare yourself to the Inca children.**

When I was eight, I had lots of paper books. Inca children didn't have any paper books. They had ... .

13 ICT 💬 **Collect information about another ancient civilisation. Create your own quiz.**

Skills in Action

Vocabulary
Places/Buildings in a town/city

1 **a)** **Look at the map, then complete the sentences.**
Use: *in front of, opposite, next to, on, between.*

1 The school is .... the park.
2 The café is .... the hotel and the restaurant.
3 The supermarket is .... the post office.
4 There's a bus stop .... the cinema.
5 The museum is .... the corner of Hill Street and King Street.

b) **Where is:** *the hospital? the bank? the petrol station? the post office? the department store? the restaurant? the train station? the hotel?* **Tell your partner.**

Listening

2 🎧 **Listen to the directions. Fill in the missing information.**

Destination: the [**1**], Hill Street
Directions: Go [**2**] King Street.
Continue straight on King Street.
In [**3**] metres, turn right onto [**4**] Street.
Continue straight for 100 metres.
Your destination is on your [**5**]

Everyday English
Asking for/Giving directions

3 **Read the dialogue and choose the correct word.**
🎧 **Listen and check.**

Amy: Excuse me, was there a police station here?
Ben: Yes, there was. It was next to the petrol station, but now it's on Oak Street.
Amy: Can you please tell me the way there?
Ben: Of course. Walk up King Street and turn **1) right/left** at the museum. Then walk up Hill Street and turn **2) right/left** at Oak Street. It's the third building on the **3) right/left** opposite the hospital.
Amy: Thank you.

4 👥 **Use the language in the box to ask for and give directions from:** *the hotel to the post office, the café to the petrol station, the cinema to the supermarket.*

Asking for directions	Giving directions
• Excuse me. Where's the ...? • How do I get to ...? • Could/Can you tell me how to get to ...? • Could/Can you tell me the way to ...?	• Go up/down… • It's on your left /right. • Turn left/right ... • It's on the corner of ... • It's next to/opposite/etc ... • Cross the street.

Pronunciation /l/ pronounced or silent

5 🎧 **Listen and circle the words in which the /l/ is silent. Listen again and repeat.**

could – field – talk – walk – clean – school

Reading & Writing

6 Read the article and put the paragraphs into the correct order.

The new Canary Wharf

A ☐ Canary Wharf was a dirty area fifty years ago. There were lots of empty warehouses but there weren't many shops. People didn't have much money or nice houses because they couldn't find jobs. Most of them didn't have cars so they had to get around by bus or on foot.

B ☐ Canary Wharf is the old port of London. Today, the area is completely different to how it was fifty years ago.

C ☐ Today, Canary Wharf has so much to offer. It is a nice place to live.

D ☐ Nowadays, Canary Wharf is much cleaner because they clean the river. There are beautiful flats and lots of shops, offices and restaurants. People have got more money and lovely houses and cars. There are three underground train stations and even an international airport.

 **Writing Tip**

Linking ideas: because/so

We use **because** to give a reason: *My neighbourhood is crowded now because more people come here to find work than in the past.*

We use **so** to show a result: *The metro is faster than the bus so lots of people prefer using it.*

7 Read the Writing Tip. Use *because* or *so* to fill in the gaps.

1 Nobody could cross the river .... there wasn't a bridge.

2 Nowadays, there is a bridge across the river .... people can cross it.

3 The streets were dark .... they didn't have electric lighting.

4 Today, there are lots of shops .... you can buy more things.

5 There weren't any buses .... people could only walk.

6 Cars couldn't go down the street .... it was very narrow.

8 Complete the notes about Canary Wharf and use them to talk about what the place was like in the past and today.

Then	Now
Canary Wharf was a **d**................. area fifty years ago.	Canary Wharf is a **c**.................. area nowadays.
There were **e**.................. warehouses. There weren't **m**............... shops.	There are **f**.................. , lots of shops, offices and restaurants.
People didn't have **m**............... money or **n**............... houses or cars.	People have got more money and **l**.................. houses and cars.
People could only get around by bus or on foot.	People can get around by **t**.................. and there is an airport.

9 **ICT** Collect information about what the place you live in was like 50 years ago. Complete a Then & Now table like the one in Ex. 8.

Writing (an article about a place then and now)

10 Use the plan below and ideas from Ex. 9 to write an article about the place you live in then and now for an international travel magazine (80-100 words). You can use the article in Ex. 6 as a model.

Plan

Title
Para 1: name of the place; location
Main Body
Para 2: what life was like then (what there was/were, there wasn't/weren't, what people didn't have and what they could/couldn't do)
Para 3: what life is like now (what there is/are, what people have got and what people can do)
Conclusion
Para 4: comments about change

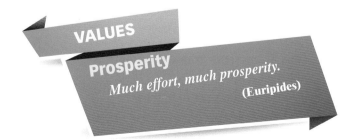

VALUES

Prosperity
Much effort, much prosperity.
(Euripides)

9 Culture

UK street names ▶ VIDEO

From Ha-Ha Road and Frying Pan Alley to streets called Bow-wow and Swing Swang Lane, the streets and roads of the UK have some very strange names. There's a No Name Street, a There and Back Again Lane and even a Whip-Ma-Whop-Ma Gate. Every street name has an interesting story behind it.

A Streets with work names

There are streets in the UK called Butchers Row and The Poultry. These streets get their names from people's jobs. For example, on Butchers Row there were lots of butchers, while on The Poultry people had lots of chickens for sale.

B Names that describe streets

UK street names can also describe what the streets were like. Walking down Long Street could take you some time. And Straight Street was just that! But High Street doesn't mean the street is higher than the others. It shows that the street had the town's most important buildings and shops.

C Royal roads

A lot of roads and streets in Britain get their names from kings and queens. There are Kings Roads, Victoria Streets and Albert Roads. Many of these names come from Britain's past kings and queens. In this way, British people could honour their royals.

CASTLE HILL

CURTAIN ROAD

PRINCE AVENUE

✓ **Check these words**

poultry, straight, royal, honour

Listening & Reading

1 Look at the signs. Where do streets in the UK get their names from?
🎧 Listen and read to find out.

2 Read the text again and explain the meaning of the street names in the photo.

Speaking & Writing

3 Use the signs to present streets in the UK and the meaning of their names.

4 ICT 💬 Work in groups. Collect information about street names in your country and their meanings. Present it to the class.

5 THINK Create your own city. Think of names to give to its streets. Present them to the class. Explain where each street gets its name from.

Vocabulary

1 **Fill in:** *stone, green, fishing, running, west.*

1 People in the village get around in .... boats.
2 Modern homes today have .... water.
3 There are some lovely old .... cottages in the area.
4 The .... coast of the country is very beautiful.
5 The fields are .... because there is so much rain.

(5 x 3 = 15)

2 **Fill in:** *busy, difficult, quiet, different, big.*

Crete is a **1)** .... island in the Mediterranean Sea. There are tourists there every summer so it's always a **2)** .... place then. But fifty years ago it was **3)** .... Life was **4)** .... and peaceful. People didn't have much money, though, so life was **5)** ....

(5 x 3 = 15)

3 **Match to form collocations.**

1	☐ bus	**A**	houses
2	☐ police	**B**	shop
3	☐ department	**C**	stop
4	☐ post	**D**	station
5	☐ souvenir	**E**	office
6	☐ ferry	**F**	centre
7	☐ sports	**G**	fields
8	☐ green	**H**	boats
9	☐ guest	**I**	airport
10	☐ international	**J**	store

(10 x 1 = 10)

Grammar

4 **Choose the correct word, then complete the short answers.**

1 **Were/was** you at the gym yesterday afternoon. No, I ....
2 Did you **have/had** a flat screen TV when you were 10? No, I ....
3 **Could/Couldn't** you swim when you were 5? Yes, I ....
4 **Were/Was** John at home last night? Yes, he ....
5 **Did/Does** he have a bike when he was 4? Yes, he ....

(5 x 4 = 20)

5 **Fill in with:** *have got, wasn't, were, couldn't, was, weren't, is, are, could, haven't got, can.*

1 Today she .... a famous film star, but when she was twenty years old she ....
2 There .... six members in the band now. Three years ago there .... only four members.
3 A: .... you play the guitar well when you were twelve?
   B: No, I ...., but I .... play it well now.
4 I .... five brothers, but I .... any sisters.
5 When I .... young, there .... any cinemas in the town.

(5 x 4 = 20)

Everyday English

6 **Complete the dialogue. Use:** *opposite, walk, excuse, turn, corner.*

A: **1)** .... me, can you tell me where the bank is?
B: Of course. **2)** .... up River Street and **3)** .... right at the bank and walk down Lake Avenue. The café is on the **4)** .... of Lake Avenue and Hay Road, **5)** .... the supermarket.
A: Thank you.

(5 x 4 = 20)
Total 100

Competences

GOOD ✓
VERY GOOD ✓ ✓
EXCELLENT ✓ ✓ ✓

Lexical Competence
Talk about
• features in a place
• places/buildings in a town/city
• transport

Reading Competence
• read for specific information (answer questions; identify meaning)
• read for coherence (order paragraphs)

Listening Competence
• listen for specific information (error correction; note taking)

Speaking Competence
• describe a place then & now
• ask for/give directions

Writing Competence
• write a text comparing two places
• write an article

Values: Respect

DESTINATIONS | BOOKING | SHOP

 ▶ VIDEO

SEARCH OK

The Traveller's Guide

It's fun to travel and see different cultures, but always remember to show respect. Here are our top tips!

Ask first

Taking photographs is the best way to remember your holiday. Just make sure you always ask before taking photos of people, or inside museums and other important buildings.

Respect the local dress code

People wear different clothes in different countries. In some cultures, it is common to cover your arms, legs or even your head when you enter a religious building. In others, you have to take off your shoes before you can enter. Make sure your clothes do not insult the locals.

Leave it how you find it

Respect isn't just for people – it's for the world around us, too. Never leave rubbish on beaches or hiking trails, and don't climb on or touch ancient ruins.

Be careful what you buy

Do not buy products made from endangered species. Buy souvenirs people make in the place you're visiting and help the local economy.

We all live on the same planet, but every country is different. Research the local culture before you travel. After all, respect costs nothing.

☆ 🏠 ✉

---

1 Look at the title of the text and the introduction. How can travellers respect local cultures?

🎧 Listen and read to find out.

2 (THINK) What is the purpose of the text? How can the information help you?

3 (THINK) 💬 How can visitors show respect in your country? Discuss in groups.

Public Speaking Skills

1 a) Read the task.

You are studying History at an American university. It is Culture Day. Present a historic landmark from your country to the other students on your course.

b) 🎧 Listen and read the model. Then copy and complete the spidergram in your notebook.

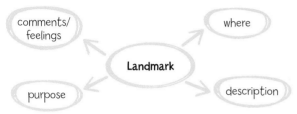

2 Read the theory. Which way to get feedback from the audience is in the model?

Study Skills

Ways to get feedback from the audience

At the end of your presentation, to check if the audience understood your talk, you can use:

- **Pop quiz style questions in teams:** Split the audience into two teams (A and B) and ask questions about the topic. *e.g. It's time for a quiz in teams! The team that gets the most correct answers wins! Team A: Where is the Eiffel Tower? ... Correct! Team B: How old is it? ...*
- **Open discussion:** Invite the audience to share their own similar experiences. *e.g. Would you like to share your experience?*
- **Polling questions:** Ask the audience a question. The audience can answer by raising their hands or standing up. *e.g. Who wants to visit Machu Picchu?*
- **Focus groups:** Divide the audience into groups of 3-4 people and give questions for them to discuss and report back. *e.g. Please get into groups of three. What impressed you most about Angkor Wat and why?*

3 ICT Copy the spidergram in Ex. 1b and complete it with information about a historic landmark from your country. Use your notes and the model to prepare and give a presentation.

Hi, I'm Nenet Reis and I have a question for you. Do you know which was the tallest building in the world for thousands of years? Well, a very long time ago the tallest building was the Great Pyramid, an important symbol of my country, Egypt.

The Great Pyramid is the biggest of the three pyramids at Giza, near Cairo in Egypt. It's 146 metres tall, 230 metres wide at the bottom, and there are over two million blocks of stone in its walls! It is also very old – 4,500 years old, in fact!

No one is sure what the Great Pyramid was for, but many people think it was a tomb for King Khufu. It's special because almost all the other pyramids in Egypt have got paintings and objects inside them, but the Great Pyramid is empty, and no one knows why.

The Great Pyramid was one of the Seven Wonders of the Ancient World, and the Egyptian people are very proud of it. It is a symbol of the start of our civilisation. In the words of Marcus Garvey, "A people without the knowledge of their past history, origin and culture is like a tree without roots." The whole of Egypt grows from the roots of its past, and that's why it's so important to learn our history!

Now, it's time for a quiz! Let's get into teams. The team that gets the most correct answers wins! Team A: Where is the Great Pyramid? ... Yes, it's in Egypt! Team B: How tall is it? ... That's right, 146 meters. Team A: How many blocks of stone are in its walls? ... You're correct, over two million! Team B: How old is it? ... 4,500 years old, that's right! Team A: What do most people think the purpose of the Great Pyramid was? ... Yes, a tomb for King Khufu. Team B: What is inside the Great Pyramid? ... That's right, nothing! ... Great – it's a draw! Well done, everyone!

Thank you for your time.

81

Their stories live on

Vocabulary: Famous people and their achievements, Jobs, Feelings/Reactions
Grammar: Past simple (regular, irregular), prepositions of movement, conjunctions, adverb formation,

Everyday English: Narrating past events
Writing: A story
A biography

Vocabulary

Jobs

1 **Match the people to the fact files.**

1 ☐ Mexican painter
(6th July 1907 – 13th July 1954)

2 ☐ German physicist & teacher
(14th March 1879 – 18th April 1955)

3 ☐ Indian politician & lawyer
(2nd October 1869 – 30th January 1948)

4 ☐ British actor & model
(14th October 1927 – 23rd May 2017)

5 ☐ Serbian inventor & engineer
(10th July 1856 – 7th January 1943)

6 ☐ American zoologist
(16th January 1932 – 26th December 1985)

> **Study Skills**
>
> **Reading dates**
> We write: 26/8/1959 or 26th August, 1959
> We say: the twenty-sixth of August, nineteen fifty-nine
> **or**
> August the twenty-sixth, nineteen fifty-nine

2 **Ask and answer questions about the people in Ex. 1, as in the example.**

A: Who was Nikola Tesla?
B: He was a Serbian inventor and engineer.
A: When was he born?
B: He was born on the 10th of July, 1856.
A: When did he die?
B: He died on the 7th of January, 1943.

Reading

3 **Read the sentences. Are they true *(T)* or false *(F)*?** 🎧 **Listen and read to find out.**

1 Roger Moore wanted to be a police officer. ....
2 Frida Kahlo always wanted to be an artist. ....
3 Albert Einstein didn't find his first job difficult. ....

4 **Read again and write *RM* for Roger Moore, *AE* for Albert Einstein or *FK* for Frida Kahlo. Then explain the words in bold.**

He/She…

1 had trouble finding a job. ....
2 had help from a parent. ....
3 was in an accident. ....
4 lost a job. ....

A. Roger Moore

B. Dian Fossey

C. Mahatma Gandhi

D. Albert Einstein

E. Nikola Tesla

F. Frida Kahlo

Making the Best of a Bad Situation

Sometimes bad luck can lead to amazing things …

Roger Moore

Roger Moore's first job was in a company making cartoons, but they **fired** him. His career changed with the help of his father. His father was a police officer, and one day he went to the house of a famous film director to **look into** a robbery. Later, he brought his son Roger, along to meet the director, and the director **offered** him a small part in his next film. A star was born!

Frida Kahlo

When she was young, Frida Kahlo wanted to be a doctor. But at the age of 18, she was on a bus when a tram crashed into it. Frida had to stay in bed for months before she was able to walk again. To pass the time, she started painting. After, Frida painted pictures of herself with special tools and mirrors. She produced some of the most beautiful self-portraits of the 20th century.

Albert Einstein

After he left university, Albert Einstein couldn't find work as a teacher at first. But he needed money, so he took a job in the Swiss Patent Office. His job was to decide if an inventor's idea was **original**. The job was easy for him, so he had plenty of time to work on his own ideas. In fact, he **came up with** his theory of relativity and the equation $E=MC^2$ there!

> ✓ **Check these words**
>
> fire, robbery, crash, theory of relativity, equation

5 Fill in *work* or *job*.

1 The engineer offered me a .... in her office.
2 After Andy left university, it took him a few months to find ....
3 Joel's father lost his .... , so he's looking for another position now.
4 My sister wants to be a model, but I told her it's hard ....
5 I'm looking for a .... as an actor.

6 Find five jobs in the text. Explain to your partner what these people do.

Speaking

7 ⟨THINK⟩ Which of the people in the text do you think was the luckiest? Why?

Writing

8 ICT 💬 ⟨THINK⟩ Hall of Fame: Choose six famous people from the past from your country. Find photos of the people and label them with their names, what job they did and their year of birth/death. Present them to the class.

Grammar in Use

J. R. R. Tolkien *(1892-1973)*

J. R. R. Tolkien was born in South Africa on 3rd January 1892. At the age of three, he went to England with his mother and brother. Unfortunately, his father died in South Africa before he could join them. His mother taught her two children at home, and Tolkien learned to love books from her. Sadly, she died too when he was 12. A friend of the family raised him and his brother. Tolkien studied English Language and Literature at Exeter College. In 1916, he married Edith Bratt, but left in the same year to fight for Britain in World War I. He left the army in 1920 and started his academic career. He also wrote stories. Tolkien began 'The Hobbit' in 1930. It made him very famous. Later, he wrote 'The Lord of the Rings'. It took him more than ten years. He died on 2nd September, 1973.

1 **a)** Read the table. Find examples in the biography.

Past simple	
Affirmative	I/You/He, etc. **watched** TV last night.
Negative	I/You/He, etc. **didn't watch** TV last night.
Interrogative	**Did** I/you/he, etc. **watch** TV last night?
Short answers	Yes, I/you/he, etc. **did**. No, I/you/he, etc. **didn't**.

We use the past simple for actions which happened in the past and won't happen again.
*Diana **married** Prince Charles in 1981.* (When? In 1981.)
Time expressions: *yesterday, ago, in 1950, last Monday/week/month,* etc.

- We add **-ed** to most regular verbs. *I work - I work**ed***
- We add **-d** to verbs ending in *-e*. *I love - I love**d***
- Verbs ending in consonant + *y* drop the *-y* and add **-ied**. *I study - I stud**ied*** **BUT** *I enjoy - I enjoy**ed***
- Other verbs have irregular forms: *say - **said**.* Look at the list of irregular verbs at the back of the book.

b) Find the past simple of the verbs below in the biography and write them down. Which are irregular?

1	go	–	*went*	**8**	marry	– ....
2	die	–		**9**	leave	– ....
3	can	–		**10**	start	– ....
4	teach	–		**11**	write	– ....
5	learn	–		**12**	begin	– ....
6	raise	–		**13**	make	– ....
7	study	–		**14**	take	– ....

2 **a)** Put the verbs in brackets into the past simple. Which verbs are irregular?

Sir Alexander Fleming **1)** .... **(be)** a famous scientist. He was born in Scotland on 6th August, 1881. He **2)** .... **(study)** Medicine at St Mary's Hospital in London. After World War I, he **3)** .... **(return)** to St Mary's and **4)** .... **(work)** there as a professor. In 1915, he **5)** .... **(marry)** Sarah Marion McElroy and they **6)** .... **(have)** a son. He **7)** .... **(discover)** penicillin in 1928 and **8)** .... **(receive)** the Nobel Prize for Medicine in 1945. His wife **9)** .... **(die)** in 1949.

Fleming married again in 1953. His second wife **10)** .... **(be)** a Greek doctor, Dr Amalia Koutsouris. Fleming **11)** .... **(die)** on 11th March, 1955. They **12)** .... **(bury)** him in St Paul's Cathedral in London.

b) Ask and answer questions about Alexander Fleming, as in the example.

1 study/Science?
   A: Did he study Science?
   B: No, he didn't. He studied Medicine.
2 work/as a doctor?
3 marry/Mary Marion McElroy?
4 have/a daughter?
5 discover/radium?
6 receive/Nobel Prize for Science?
7 die/in 1965?

3 Look at the facts about Elvis Presley and say what he did/didn't do, as in the example.

1 live/in New York (✗)
   Elvis Presley didn't live in New York.
2 get first guitar/eleventh birthday (✓)
3 record/first hit/1954 (✓)
4 write/his own songs (✗)
5 make/31 films (✓)
6 perform concerts/in Europe (✗)

4 SPEAKING **Use the prompts and the time expressions below and, in pairs, act out short dialogues, as in the example.**

travel abroad?

post a video online?

When was the last time you ...

go shopping?

get a gift?

update your social media profile?

lend money to a friend?

eat at a restaurant?

meet a famous person?

yesterday

yesterday morning/evening, etc.

two days/weeks, etc. ago

last Monday/Tuesday, etc.

a week/month, etc. ago

A: *When was the last time you travelled abroad?*
B: *The last time I travelled abroad was two years ago. How about you?*
A: *The last time I travelled abroad was a month ago.*

5 **First, put the verbs in brackets into the past simple. Then, match 1-6 with a-f to make sentences.**

A

1 ◯ Steven Paul Jobs was born in California, USA in 1955. His parents .... **(give)** him up at birth

2 ◯ Jobs .... **(meet)** Steve Wozniak at work in 1971

3 ◯ Wozniak .... **(design)** a computer in 1976

4 ◯ Their company .... **(be)** successful

5 ◯ Jobs .... **(return)** to computers in 1997

6 ◯ Steve Jobs .... **(die)** in 2011, and

B

a and they .... **(become)** good friends.

b and he .... **(lead)** the company to greater success.

c by then his company .... **(be)** one of the most successful in the world.

d and Paul and Clara Jobs .... **(adopt)** him.

e but Jobs .... **(leave)** and bought a film-making company.

f and Jobs .... **(agree)** to help him sell it.

Prepositions of movement

6 **Look at the pictures and use the prepositions to fill in the gaps in the text. Then, put the pictures in the correct order. Finally, look at the pictures and tell the story. Start like this:** *Ralph went horse-riding in the countryside.*

a ◯ past   **b** ◯ towards   **c** ◯ across

d ◯ up/down   **e** ◯ along   **f** ◯ under

g ◯ into   **h** ◯ through   **i** ◯ over

It was a lovely day, so Ralph decided to go for a ride in the countryside. He got on his horse and rode out of the field. At first, everything was fine. He went **1)** *along* a road, **2)** .... a tunnel and **3)** .... a forest. Then, he went **4)** .... a hill. The view from there was beautiful! After that, he went **5)** .... the other side of the hill, **6)** .... a little old cottage and **7)** .... a bridge. After that, he went **8)** .... a field. Suddenly, everything went wrong! A tractor scared the horse and it jumped **9)** .... a fence. Ralph fell off the horse and **10)** .... a lake. He got very wet! It was a horrible experience!

7 👥 **Use the pictures in Ex. 6 to tell the story again, but make three mistakes. Your partner corrects you.**

Skills in Action

Vocabulary
Feelings/Reactions

1 a) 🎧 Listen and repeat. Which are positive/ negative feelings?

1 frightened

2 happy

3 upset

4 worried

5 shocked

6 excited

7 proud

8 confused

b) 👥 You've got two minutes. Make as many sentences as you can using the adjectives in Ex. 1a.

I watched a horror film last night. I felt frightened.

Listening

2 a) 🎧 Listen to the sounds. What do you think the story is about?

b) 🎧 Listen to the story. Put the events into the order they happened (1-8).

Claire and Greg went to a wildlife park.	*1*
They climbed into the ranger's truck.	....
The car wouldn't start.	....
The lions scared Claire.	....
Smoke and flames came out of the engine.	....
They tried to attract someone's attention.	....
A ranger scared away the lions.	....
They stopped to take pictures of lions.	....

Everyday English
Narrating an event

3 Read the dialogue and put the verbs in the past simple.

🎧 Listen and check.

> **Andy:** Hello, Sally. How was your weekend in London? **1)** .... **(you/enjoy)** it?
>
> **Sally:** Hey, Andy. Yes, I **2)** .... **(have)** a great time. It was fantastic. And guess who I **3)** .... **(meet)**! Liam Hemsworth, the famous Hollywood actor!
>
> **Andy:** I don't believe it! He's your favourite! How **4)** .... **(that/happen)**?
>
> **Sally:** I was outside the museum when I **5)** .... **(see)** him.
>
> **Andy:** What **6)** .... **(you/do)**?
>
> **Sally:** I **7)** .... **(go)** up to him and **8)** .... **(ask)** him for a selfie with him. Here, take a look.
>
> **Andy:** That's amazing! You're so lucky!

4 👥👥 Tell your partner about how you spent last weekend. Use sentences from the Useful Language box.

A: How was your weekend?
B: It was amazing ... etc.

Narrating an event	
Asking	**Responding**
• How was your weekend? • What was it like?/Did you enjoy it? • That's terrible/amazing! • What happened? • Really?/ I don't believe it!	• It was great/amazing/ fantastic/amusing. • I didn't like it much./It was awful/boring. • Guess what happened to me/who I met, etc.

Intonation in *yes/no* questions

5 🎧 Listen and repeat.

> ***Yes/No*** questions: rising intonation
> *Did you have a nice time?* ↗

1 Is he an actor?
2 Did she act in films?
3 Did you study Art?
4 Did you know him?

Reading & Writing

> **Joining sentences**
> We can join sentences with words such as **and**, **but**, **because**, **so**, **then**, **when**, etc.
> Study the examples:
> *She stood up **and** walked towards the door.*
> *He looked, **but** he couldn't see anything.*
> *He closed the window **because** it was very cold.*
> *It was very late, **so** he decided to go home.*
> *He opened the door, **then** turned on the lights.*
> *He was in bed **when** he heard a strange noise.*

6 Read the theory, then read the story and choose the correct linking word.

It was a beautifully warm autumn day **1) because/and** Billy was on his way to college. He was near the entrance **2) when/so** he saw his close friend Tania. He waved to her, **3) so/but** she didn't see him. She had headphones on and her head was down. She started to cross the wide road.

"Stop!" shouted Billy loudly, **4) because/then** he suddenly saw a red car coming fast along the road. Tania had headphones on, **5) but/so** she couldn't hear Billy's frightened cry. Billy ran quickly towards her and got there just before the car. He grabbed Tania's arm hard, **6) then/when** pulled her out of the way of the car. The car whizzed past them both, missing them by inches.

Tania's face was pale **7) because/and** she looked shocked. "I think you just saved my life, Billy," she said in a low voice.

"That's what friends are for," said Billy happily.

7 Find the adjectives the writer uses in the story to describe the following:

• day • friend • road • cry • face • voice

8 Write the adverbs formed from the adjectives. What adverbs did the writer use in the story in Ex. 6? What adjectives do they come from?

Adjective	Adverb	Adjective	Adverb
hard	....	fast	....
strange	....	easy	....
happy	....	good	....
desperate	....	quick	....

Writing (a story)

9 **a)** Look at the picture and read the text. Answer the questions.

> That cold winter afternoon, I decided to take my dog, Rex, for a walk on the beach. Suddenly, Rex began to bark loudly.

1 When did this happen?
2 What was the weather like?
3 Where did this happen?
4 Who was there?
5 What happened first?

b) 🎧 Listen and put the events in the correct order (1-6).

A	I saw a boy in the sea.	....
B	We brought the boy back home.	....
C	The nanny thanked me.	....
D	I brought the boy back to shore.	....
E	I dived into the water.	....
F	The woman called for help.	*1*

10 Use the ideas in Ex. 9 to write your story for an international magazine's short story competition (80-100 words). Follow the plan.

> **Plan**
> **Para 1:** time/place the event happened; weather; people; what happened first
> **Para 2:** events in the order they happened
> **Para 3:** what happened in the end; how people felt

VALUES

Responsibility
You must be the change you wish to see in the world.
(M. Gandhi)

 ▶ VIDEO

ೋ William Shakespeare ೋ
A Poet for All Time

"Fame lives long," wrote William Shakespeare, and in his case, this was definitely true.

William Shakespeare was born in Stratford-upon-Avon in 1564. His family were simple people. His father sold leather and his mother **cared for** the family. We do not know much about Shakespeare's **childhood**. It is possible he went to the local grammar school – King Edward VI School. Life in Stratford was peaceful and quiet. In 1582, he married Anne Hathaway and they had three children: Susanna was born in 1583 and the **twins**, Hamnet and Judith, were born in 1585.

In 1592, Shakespeare moved to London. It was a large, noisy and exciting city. He **joined** the Lord Chamberlain's Men – a company of actors – and soon began acting and writing plays. These include historical plays like *Henry V*, tragedies like *Romeo and Juliet* and comedies like *As You Like It*.

Shakespeare died in 1616, but not before he gave the world 42 plays, wrote hundreds of poems, and changed the English language **forever**. He added about 1,700 words to the English language as well as many **common** phrases, like "a heart of gold" and "All's well that ends well." His works continue to inspire readers even to the present day.

Listening & Reading

1 **How are these names related to Shakespeare?**
Stratford-upon-Avon – Anne Hathaway – Susanna – Hamnet and Judith – London – the Lord Chamberlain's Men – Henry V – Romeo and Juliet.
🎧 Listen and read to find out.

2 **Read the text again and decide if the statements are** *T* **(True),** *F* **(False) or** *DS* **(Doesn't say).**

1 William Shakespeare had three brothers. ....
2 His mother worked with his father. ....
3 King Edward VI School was in Stratford-upon-Avon. ....
4 Shakespeare had three sons. ....
5 Shakespeare didn't like his birthplace. ....
6 In London, he worked as an actor. ....

3 **Explain the meaning of the words in bold. Check in your dictionary.**

✓ **Check these words**
definitely, leather, inspire

Speaking & Writing

4 ☁THINK☁ **William Shakespeare is an important figure in the English language. Why?**

5 ICT  **Collect information about an important writer from your country. Think about:** *name – what famous for – when/where born – early years – studies – family – achievements – when/where died.* **Write a short article for an international magazine (80-100 words). Read your article to the class.**

Vocabulary

1 **Fill in:** *zoologist, painter, actor, physicist, politician, lawyer.*

1 Abraham Lincoln was an American .... and the 16th President of the United States.
2 Noah Schnapp is my favourite .... in the TV series *Stranger Things*.
3 He wants to be a(n) .... because he loves animals.
4 Albert Einstein was a(n) .... He is famous for his theories about space and time.
5 She is a(n) .... and represents people in court.
6 *The Persistence of Memory* is the most famous picture by Spanish .... Salvador Dali.

(6 x 2 = 12)

2 **Choose the correct word.**

1 It was very dark and Angela was **shocked/ frightened**.
2 Jimmy is **proud/upset** because he won the competition.
3 The twins are flying to Switzerland and they're so **confused/excited**!
4 Max's sister keeps taking his CDs, so he's very **upset/happy**.
5 My brother has a hard exam tomorrow, and he's **worried/excited**.
6 Joe's sister was **proud/shocked** when she saw the car accident.

(6 x 2 = 12)

Grammar

3 **Write the** *past simple* **form of the verbs below.**

1 marry – ....
2 care – ....
3 make – ....
4 watch – ....
5 take – ....
6 die – ....
7 enjoy – ....
8 say – ....

(8 x 2 = 16)

4 **Put the verbs in brackets in the** *past simple*.

1 When was the last time you ....**(feel)** scared?
2 .... **(they/fly)** to Malta last month?
3 He .... **(write)** 42 poems.
4 He .... **(travel)** all over Asia before he moved to Los Angeles.
5 They .... **(not/play)** our favourite song at the concert yesterday.
6 The last time he .... **(watch)** a performance was two weeks ago.
7 Alice .... **(not/pass)** the History test yesterday.
8 Where .... **(he/work)** in 2015?
9 Why .... **(he/leave)** early yesterday?
10 He .... **(go)** to the theatre last Saturday.

(10 x 2 = 20)

5 **Fill in the gaps in the table.**

adjective	adverb
sudden	1) ....
2)	beautifully
fast	3) ....
happy	4) ....
5)	well

(5 x 4 = 20)

Everyday English

6 **Match the sentences.**

1 ☐ How was your weekend in London?
2 ☐ I met a famous singer!
3 ☐ What did you do?
4 ☐ What happened next?
5 ☐ I had a car accident!

A I asked her for her autograph.
B Then I took a selfie with her.
C That's amazing!
D It was fantastic.
E How terrible!

(5 x 4 = 20)

Total 100

Competences

GOOD ✓
VERY GOOD ✓ ✓
EXCELLENT ✓ ✓ ✓

Lexical Competence
Talk about:
• famous people and their achievements
• jobs
• feelings/reactions

Reading Competence
• read for specific information (multiple matching; T/F statements; multiple matching; T/F/DS statements)

Listening Competence
• listen for detail (order events)
Speaking Competence
• narrate past events
Writing Competence
• write a story
• write a biography

Time will tell

Vocabulary: The environment, Helping the environment, Summer plans
Grammar: should/shouldn't, future simple/be going to/present continuous (future meaning), it – there
Everyday English: Inviting – Accepting/Refusing
Writing: An email about your summer plans

Vocabulary
The environment

1 Which of these predictions do you think/don't you think will come true in 50 years' time?

I think people will recycle all their rubbish.
I don't think wild animals will disappear.

Wild animals will disappear.

There will be more pollution from cars.

The rainforests will disappear.

Everyone will have electric cars.

There will be lots of rubbish.

People will live in smart houses.

People will recycle all their rubbish.

People will plant more trees.

Reading

2 Which of the predictions from Ex. 1 are there in the text?

🎧 Listen and read to find out.

🏠 Home   @ Connect   # Discover   👤 N

Andy Brown
View my profile page

89 POSTS   **119** FOLLOWING   **142** FOLLOWERS

A Dark Future or a Bright One?

3 Read the text and complete the sentences. Then, explain the words in bold.

1 According to the TV programme, some wild animals ....

2 Andy wants to start ....

3 Ben believes electric cars will solve the problem ....

4 Kelly thinks that people need to learn ....

Hi, followers! I watched a great TV programme about the environment last night. It was interesting – but it was really **sad**! We all know about pollution from cars, don't we? Well, in the future it will get worse and worse. There will be lots of people on Earth and they will make lots of rubbish. Plus, the rainforests will disappear and some of our favourite **wild** animals, like the tiger and the rhino, will disappear, too.

I was pretty miserable after that programme finished, I can tell you! But then I started thinking... maybe I can help to stop this. So I'm going to start an environmental club at my university. We're going to talk about environmental problems and do activities like **planting** trees to help the world around us.

It's **up to** us to decide if our future will be a dark one or a bright one. What are you going to do to help? Leave a comment!

Comments

Ben Smith

Hello, Andy. Love your blog! But actually, I don't think **pollution** from cars will be a problem in the future. I think everyone will have electric cars. In fact, my uncle is buying an electric car next month. I hope he'll let me drive it!

Kelly Jones

Great post, Andy! You're right, in the future, there will be lots of people on Earth. But I think we'll learn to **recycle** all our rubbish. I'm going to make sure all my family and friends will recycle everything!

Check these words

miserable, environmental club

Speaking

4 **THINK** What will you do to make our future a bright one? Tell your partner.

Vocabulary

Helping the environment

5 **Match the advice to the reasons.**

6 ways to save the planet

Advice
1 ☐ Turn off lights.
2 ☐ Use cloth shopping bags.
3 ☐ Buy food from the market.
4 ☐ Give old clothes to charity.
5 ☐ Walk or ride a bike.
6 ☐ Have a shower, not a bath.

Reasons
a It saves water.
b Cars cause pollution.
c Clothes don't end up in the rubbish.
d It saves electricity.
e Plastic bags are bad for the environment.
f It doesn't have plastic packaging.

Giving Advice
We use **should** to say what the right/best thing to do is.
You should use public transport. (= It's a good idea.)
We use **shouldn't** to say what isn't the right/best thing to do.
You shouldn't use plastic bags. (= It isn't a good idea.)
We can also give advice with: **Why don't you...? I think it's a good idea to ..., I don't think it's a good idea to ...**
Why don't you use public transport?
I think it's a good idea to use public transport.
I don't think it's a good idea to use plastic bags.

6 **Use the sentences in Ex. 5 to make sentences, as in the example.**

You should turn off the lights. It saves electricity. Why don't you ...?

Writing (a leaflet)

7 **ICT Collect more ideas on helping the environment. Use your ideas to write a leaflet to hand out at college. Use** should **or** shouldn't.

Grammar in Use

Tania: Hey, Charlie. How are you? Are you going to the gym this afternoon?

Charlie: Hi, Tania! No, I'm not going to the gym. I'm attending a presentation in the Environmental Science department.

Tania: What presentation?

Charlie: It's about green careers.

Tania: What's that?

Charlie: It's about jobs that protect our environment. You know that in the future, there won't be enough food and clean water for everyone. Well, there are people working to fix these problems. I'm going to get a job like that when I leave university.

Tania: That sounds interesting. I'll come with you!

Charlie: Great. The presentation starts at 5 pm, but there will be lots of people, so let's meet at 4:45 outside the library.

Tania: OK!

1 **Read the theory. Find examples in the dialogue.**

---
will

Affirmative: I/you/he etc. will leave.
Negative: I/you/he etc. won't leave.
Interrogative: Will I/you/he etc. leave?
Short Answers: Yes, I/you/he etc. will./No, I/you/he etc. won't.
We use **will**:
- to make predictions: *In 100 years' time, we will live in underwater cities.*
- to make on-the-spot decisions: *I'll have soup first, then steak and chips.*
Time expressions: tomorrow, soon, next week/month/etc., the day after tomorrow, etc.

---

2 **Read the examples and say: a) which are predictions; b) which are on-the-spot decisions.**

1 I'm cold. I'll close the window.
2 In 50 years' time, I think there will be more cars in the streets than people.
3 It will be cold and rainy tomorrow.
4 I'm hungry. I'll make myself a sandwich.
5 In 100 years' time, people will have flying cars.

3 **Fill in with** *will* **or** *won't*.

1 A: Sorry, Tim. We *won't* be able to help you plant trees tomorrow.
  B: It's OK. I *will* ask someone else for help.
2 A: .... it rain tomorrow?
  B: Yes, it .... Let's stay at home.
3 A: I don't think people .... live on Mars in 50 years.
  B: No, but there .... be people on the Moon.
4 A: Do you think they .... have robots to clean the seas someday?
  B: In my opinion, they .... But then again, you never know.
5 A: It's getting cold. I .... put the heating on.
  B: Great! Then I .... need to put a jumper on.

4 **a)** **What will life be like in 30 years? Read the sentences, then listen and put a** *W* **for the woman's predictions, and a** *M* **for the man's. Where nobody makes a prediction, put an** *X*.

1 People will travel in flying cars. ....
2 People will live in underwater cities. ....
3 Life will be more expensive. ....
4 People will go on holiday to the Moon. ....
5 There will be more people in the world. ....
6 Pollution will be worse. ....
7 There won't be enough trees. ....
8 People will use oxygen masks to breathe. ....
9 There will be food pills instead of fresh food. ....

b) **Ask and answer questions. Use the ideas above.**

A: *Will people travel in flying cars?*
B: *Yes, they will./No, they won't.*

5 **Read the prompts and match them to the correct on-the-spot decisions, then make sentences, as in the example.**

On-the-spot decisions

I'm thirsty.	close the window
It's raining.	have a sandwich
It's cold.	have a glass of water
I'm tired.	call the fire brigade
I'm hungry.	go to bed
It's hot.	open the window
The house is on fire.	put on my raincoat

I'm thirsty. I'll have a glass of water.

6 Read the theory. Find an example in the dialogue on p. 92. Does the example express: *a future plan*? *an intention*? *a prediction based on evidence*?

be going to

Affirmative	I am/You are/He is, etc. going to move house.
Negative	I'm not/You aren't/He isn't, etc. going to move house.
Interrogative	Am I/Are you/Is he, etc. going to move house?
Short answers	Yes, I am/you are/he is, etc. No, I'm not/you aren't/he isn't, etc.

We use **be going to** to talk about:
- future plans: *I am going to visit Poland next summer.*
- intentions: *I am going to study for a test tonight.*
- predictions based on evidence: *It's cloudy. It's going to rain*

7 a) Complete the sentences. Use the correct form of *be going to* and the verbs in the list.

• visit • go • have • play • watch • take • study

This weekend ...
John *isn't going to play* football. (✗)

1 Stan .... a film. (✓)
2 I .... my cousin in New York. (✓)
3 Jo .... a meal with Sam. (✗)
4 Michael and Tom .... for their French exam. (✗)
5 Peter .... the dog to the vet's. (✓)
6 Tania .... to a concert. (✗)

b) Ask and answer questions as in the example.

A: *Is John going to play football this weekend?*
B: *No, he isn't.*

8 Read the theory. How do these two tenses differ? Find examples of the present continuous for fixed future arrangements in the dialogue on p. 92.

be going to – present continuous

We use **be going to** to talk about **future plans** and **intentions**: *I am going to watch a DVD this afternoon.* We use the **present continuous** to talk about **fixed future arrangements**: *I am seeing my dentist this afternoon* or actions happening now/around the time of speaking *I'm having a lesson now*.

9 Look at Tom's arrangements, then, in pairs, ask and answer questions, as in the example.

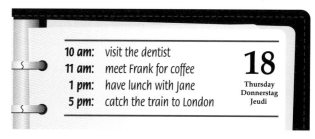

10 am: visit the dentist
11 am: meet Frank for coffee
1 pm: have lunch with Jane
5 pm: catch the train to London

18
Thursday
Donnerstag
Jeudi

A: *What is Tom doing at ten o'clock?*
B: *He's visiting the dentist at ten o'clock.*

10 Put the verbs in brackets into the future simple, *be going to* or the present continuous. Identify the uses.

1 I think we .... **(have)** our own robots in the future.
2 Mark .... **(work)** as a programmer after college.
3 Sue .... **(start)** university in October.
4 I think this year .... **(be)** better than last year.
5 I'm tired – I .... **(not/work)** late tonight.
6 They .... **(leave)** on the 10 o'clock train.
7 She is running very fast. She .... **(win)** the race.
8 They .... **(not/stay)** at Paul's this week.

11 Read the theory. Find an example in the dialogue on p. 92. Then fill in the gaps with *It* or *There*.

It –There

We use:
It will be + adjective *It will be hot in the future.*
There will be + noun *There will be flying cars soon.*

1 .... will be foggy in Dublin tomorrow.
2 .... will be strong winds in Harare tomorrow.
3 .... will be rainy in Seoul tomorrow.
4 .... will be sunny in Sydney tomorrow.
5 .... will be snow in Warsaw tomorrow.

12 **WRITING** **THINK** Write three sentences about what you think will happen in 50 years, two sentences about what you're going to do next year, and one sentence about what you're doing tonight.

Skills in Action

Vocabulary
Summer plans

1 a) Look at the pictures. Which of the following is Mary going to do in the summer? Look and say.

move house (✗)

have French lessons (✗)

start a computer course (✓)

go windsurfing (✓)

go hiking (✗)

work part-time in an animal sanctuary (✓)

join a gym (✗)

volunteer for an environmental group (✓)

b) What are you going to do this summer?

Listening

2 🎧 Listen to a dialogue and for questions 1-4 choose the correct answer (A, B or C).

1 This summer, Tim is NOT going to ...
   A plant trees. B volunteer. C make money.

2 Tim is doing a ...
   A computer course.   C cooking course.
   B language course.

3 Ken wants to do a lot of ...
   A windsurfing. B study. C relaxing.

4 How many days is Ken going to stay at the hotel for?
   A two B five C six

Everyday English
Inviting – Accepting/Refusing invitations

3 🎧 What are Emily and Lyn going to do on Sunday? Listen and read to find out.

Emily: Hey Lyn, are you busy this Saturday? I'm going to my cousin's wedding. <u>Would you like to</u> come with me?

Lyn: <u>I'd love to, but I can't.</u> I'll be in York for the weekend. I'm leaving tomorrow. Sorry!

Emily: <u>That's all right.</u> When are you coming back?

Lyn: Sunday afternoon.

Emily: <u>Why don't we</u> meet for dinner Sunday evening?

Lyn: <u>Sure, why not!</u> I'll call you when I'm back on Sunday and we can arrange where to meet.

Emily: Brilliant! Right, have to run. Have a safe trip.

Lyn: Thanks.

4 Replace the underlined phrases/sentences with phrases/sentences from the language box.

Inviting	Accepting
• Would you like to ...?	• That's a great idea!
• Can you ...?	• Sounds good/great.
• Why don't we/you ...?	• Sure, why not!
• Do you want to ...?	• I'd love to.
Refusing	**Reacting to a refusal**
• Sorry, I can't.	• That's a pity!
• I'm afraid I can't.	• Never mind!
• I'd love to, but I can't.	• That's all right.

5 👥 Use the prompts to act out a dialogue similar to the one in Ex. 3. Use phrases from the language box. Record yourselves.

A invite your friend to go to the mall on Saturday afternoon / to go to the cinema on Sunday evening

B invite your friend to go to the museum on Saturday morning / to go to the market on Saturday afternoon

Pronunciation '*ll – won't*

6 🎧 Listen and repeat.

• I'll call you. • I won't call you. • It'll be hot today.
• We won't allow it. • They won't go. • They'll come.

Reading & Writing

7 Read the email and complete the table.

Inbox 🏠 | Contacts 📞 | Log out ⤵   ✖

To: Sarah19xx@fastmail.com
Subject: holiday news

Hi Sarah,

How are you? I'm so excited about you coming to visit me this summer! I've got some fantastic plans for us.

I know your flight is landing in Poznań on 25ᵗʰ June. I can't wait to show you around my university town and introduce you to my friends. Then, after the end of term on 1st July, we're going to travel to my hometown, Wroclaw. I want you to meet my family. I'm also going to show you around the city because it's a very interesting place. Then, in August, the real summer holidays are going to start!

First, we're going to go hiking with my friends Basia and Marta in Tatra National Park because it's beautiful there! Then, we're going to join my family in Sopot to relax a bit. Sopot has got some lovely beaches and you can even try windsurfing.

I'm sure we'll have a great time. See you soon!

Love,

Lena

PLANS/INTENTIONS	REASON/PURPOSE
they/travel to *Wroclaw*	Lena wants Sarah to *meet her family*
Lena/show Sarah	it's a ....
they/go hiking in	it's very ....
they/join her family in	Lena wants to ....
....	

FIXED ARRANGEMENTS
Sarah's flight/land on ....

Writing Tip

Expressing Reason, Result or Purpose
• We express reason with **because** and result with **so**.
• We also express reason or purpose with **to**-infinitive (infinitive of purpose).
*He's going to join a gym **because** he wants to lose weight.*
*He wants to lose weight, **so** he's going to join a gym.*
*He's going to join a gym **to lose** weight.*

8 👥 Talk about Lena's plans/intentions. Use *because* or *to-infinitive* to join the sentences.

*She is going to travel back to Wroclaw **because** she wants Sarah to meet her family.*

9 Match Tony's intentions to their results, then make sentences, as in the example.

Intentions	Results
1 save money	**a** do something exciting
2 join a gym	**b** help people
3 have French lessons	**c** go on holiday
4 go windsurfing	**d** get fit
5 volunteer for a charity	**e** learn a new language

Tony is going to save money so he can go on holiday.

Writing (an email about your summer plans)

10 **a)** Think about your summer holidays. Copy the table in Ex. 7 in your notebook and complete it.

b) Use your notes in Ex. 10a to write an email to an English-speaking friend who is going to spend the summer with you, saying what you are going to do together. (80-100 words). Follow the plan.

Plan

Hi + *(your friend's first name)*
Para 1: reason for writing the email
Para 2, 3: your plans & intentions with reasons
Para 4: closing remarks (e.g. *See you soon.*)
Best,
(your first name)

VALUES

Change *A change is as good as a rest.* (saying)

▶ VIDEO

Give a Little Time to the Trees

Arbor Day started in 1872 in Nebraska, USA. It is a special day to support the planting of trees. A hundred years later, in 1972, John Rosenow started a charity and education organisation to inspire people all over the USA to plant, **care for**, and celebrate trees. Today, every state celebrates Arbor Day and the Arbor Day Foundation is the biggest tree planting organisation in the world.

The Arbor Day Foundation does **amazing** work. They raise money and work hard to plant trees in towns and cities. They also look after national forests, replant trees after natural disasters, and help young people learn about trees and connect with the natural world.

Supporters and volunteers are very important to the work of the Arbor Day Foundation. People can **volunteer** to help plant trees. They can also organise or take part in fundraising events, or make a donation.

If you would like to find out more about how you can support the Arbor Day Foundation, please visit www.arborday.org

Listening & Reading

1 **Read the title of the text and look at the picture. What do you think the Arbor Day Foundation does?**
🎧 **Listen and read to find out.**

2 **Read the text quickly. What is the purpose of the text?**

3 **Read the text again. Mark the statements (1-3) as *T* (true), *F* (false) or *DS* (doesn't say).**

1 Arbor Day started in Nebraska. ....
2 John Rosenow is from Nebraska. ....
3 Volunteers can only plant trees. ....

✓ **Check these words**

inspire, fundraising event, donation, support

4 **Explain the words in bold.**

5 ⟨THINK⟩ **Would you like to join the Arbor Day Foundation? Why/Why not?**

Speaking & Writing

6 ICT 💬 **Collect information about a charity in your country. Make notes under the headings: *name of organisation – history of organisation – activities*. Present the charity to the class.**

Vocabulary

1 Match the words to make phrases.

1	☐ wild	a	paper
2	☐ shopping	b	programme
3	☐ recycled	c	bag
4	☐ smart	d	group
5	☐ TV	e	animal
6	☐ environmental	f	house
7	☐ public	g	car
8	☐ electric	h	transport

(8 x 2 = 16)

2 Fill in: *join, volunteer, go, work, have, move, recycle, save, give, plant.*

1 I want to ……………….. French lessons this summer.
2 I'm not very fit – I'm going to …..…………… a gym.
3 How much of your rubbish do you …………………?
4 Dad wants to …………… house to be closer to Gran.
5 We all must act to ……………………… the planet!
6 I …………………… part-time in a shop.
7 Michael can't …...............…………… windsurfing this weekend.
8 I don't earn money when I ………………………, but I feel good.
9 We're meeting at 10 in the park to …………………… trees.
10 I'm going to ……………………… my old clothes to charity.

(10 x 2 = 20)

3 Fill in: *computer, plastic, environmental, animal, cloth, summer.*

1 He spends his weekends working at a(n) ………………… sanctuary.
2 I always use ……………… bags, not plastic ones.
3 Are you doing a(n) ……………… course?
4 Fruit in supermarkets has got a lot of ……………… packaging.
5 Sarah volunteers for a(n) …………………………… group.
6 Where are you going on your ……………… holidays?

(6 x 3 = 18)

Grammar

4 Rewrite the sentences using *should* or *shouldn't*.

1 It's a good idea for us to recycle.
………………………………………………………………………
2 Don't throw cans into the bin.
………………………………………………………………………
3 It's not a good idea for Sally to leave her job.
………………………………………………………………………
4 Turn the heating down.
………………………………………………………………………
5 Don't go out without a coat.
………………………………………………………………………

(5 x 2 = 10)

5 Choose the correct item.

1 Joan has a bucket because she **will wash/is going to wash** the car.
2 Clean up your room. Your cousin **will come/is coming** to stay tomorrow.
3 I don't think it**'ll be/'s going to be** very hot this summer.
4 John **is studying/is going to study** harder next year – he promised.
5 They don't have pizza, so what **will you order/are you ordering**?
6 Terrence **is going to work/is working** with computers after college.
7 **It/There** will be windy tomorrow.
8 **It/There** will be a new teacher for Biology tomorrow.

(8 x 2 = 16)

Everyday English

6 Match the exchanges.

1	☐ Would you like to come to my house for dinner?	A	Brilliant! Speak soon!
2	☐ A trip to the cinema sounds good.	B	Great! Let's meet there at 8.
3	☐ I'll call you to arrange where to meet.	C	Yes. Why don't you come?
4	☐ Are you going windsurfing next weekend?	D	I'd love to.
5	☐ I'm sorry, I can't come to your barbecue.	E	That's a pity!

(5 x 4 = 20)
Total 100

Competences

GOOD ✓
VERY GOOD ✓ ✓
EXCELLENT ✓ ✓ ✓

Lexical Competence
Talk about:
• the environment
• helping the environment
• summer plans

Reading Competence
• read for detail (sentence completion, T/F/DS statements)

Listening Competence
• listen for detail (multiple choice questions)

Speaking Competence
• give advice
• invite – accept/refuse invitations

Writing Competence
• write a leaflet
• write an email about my summer plans

Vocabulary: holiday activities, travel experiences
Grammar: present perfect, present perfect vs past simple, *The*

Everyday English: describing a holiday experience
Writing: A blog comment about a holiday experience

Take a break

Vocabulary

Holiday activities

1 **Fill in:** *ride, go, visit, see, buy (x2), take, try*.
🎧 **Listen and check.**

2 **Which of these activities did you do when you last went on holiday? Tell your partner. You can use your own ideas.**

Last July I went to … . I saw ancient buildings and tried local dishes. I swam in the sea and took lots of photos. etc.

Reading & Listening

3 **Read the text quickly. Which title is appropriate?**
Mystical Egypt – Exotic Morocco – Beautiful Mongolia.

4 **Read the sentences.**
🎧 **Then listen to and read the email Jack sent to his friend and decide if the sentences are** *T* **(True) or** *F* **(False).**

1 He has already visited the Marrakech market. ....
2 He has been to a traditional restaurant. ....
3 He has visited the museum. ....
4 He has been to Rabat. ....

✅ **Check these words**

try, spices, palace, exhibit

3 .... ancient temples

4 .... handmade souvenirs

5 .... a market

6 .... traditional dishes

7 .... spices

1 .... a camel

2 .... photos

VIDEO

8 .... sightseeing

EMAIL   LOGIN   SIGN UP   HOME

Hi Terry,

Greetings from Morocco! The weather's very hot. I've been here since Monday and I'm having a wonderful time. I'm staying with my friend, Mohammed. He lives in Marrakech. Marrakech is famous for its beautiful buildings, palaces and its market. I've already been to the market. We visited it on Tuesday. You can't imagine how noisy and crowded it was! I bought some lovely handmade souvenirs there. I even rode a camel in the desert outside Marrakech yesterday. It was fun! I've also been to a traditional restaurant. Mohammed took me there last night. I tried tagine, a Moroccan dish with chicken, fruit, vegetables and spices. The place was fantastic and the food was just delicious.

There are a lot of things I haven't done yet. I haven't been to the palaces yet, and I haven't visited the museum.

We are going on a day trip to Casablanca tomorrow and we are going to visit the museum one of these days to see the exhibits. We are also going to visit Rabat, Morocco's capital city.

Morocco is a fascinating country — you must visit it one day! Anyway, I'm returning to England on Sunday next week, so I'll call you then.

Best wishes,

Jack

---

5 **Tell your partner three false statements based on the text. Your partner corrects them.**

A: *It's raining in Morocco.*
B: *No, it isn't raining. It's hot.*

---

6 **Replace the adjectives in bold with their opposites. Check in your dictionary.**

- disgusting • cold • quiet • horrible • empty
- modern

1 I'm having a **wonderful** time.

2 The market was **noisy** and **crowded**.

3 We've been to a **traditional** restaurant.

4 The food was **delicious**.

5 The weather is very **hot**.

7 **Fill in the missing prepositions, then use them to make sentences based on the text.**

- for • to • on (x2) • with • in

1 stay .... my friend   **4** .... Tuesday
2 live .... Marrakesh   **5** go .... a day trip
3 famous ....   **6** return .... England

Speaking

8 **Read the email again, then copy the table in your notebook and complete it.**

ACTIVITIES HE DID	WHEN	WHAT HE DID THERE	WHAT IT WAS LIKE
visited the market	*Tuesday*	*bought souvenirs*	*noisy & crowded*

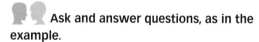 **Ask and answer questions, as in the example.**

A: *Did Jack visit the market?*
B: *Yes, he did.*
A: *When did he visit it?*
B: *On Tuesday.*
A: *What did he do there?*
B: *He bought some souvenirs.*
A: *What was it like?*
B: *It was noisy and crowded.*

Writing

9 THINK Write three reasons why you would like to visit Morocco. Read them to the class. Find someone who has the same reason(s) as you.

Grammar in Use

A: Welcome to Orlando. Have you stayed in our hotel before?

B: Yes, we have. We were here in 2002.

A: Have you visited Walt Disney World?

B: Yes, we went there on our first trip. We've also seen Universal Studios, but we haven't been to Discovery Cove yet.

A: Oh, you should go! Have you ever swum with dolphins? It's a wonderful experience!

B: Swimming with dolphins! Wow! I haven't tried anything like that before!

A: Have you booked tickets?

B: No, we haven't.

A: I can book them for you here at the hotel. I think they've got an offer on this week.

B: Thanks! That would be great! But not for today. We've driven down from New York and we're tired.

1 Read the table. Find examples in the dialogue.

Present perfect	
Affirmative	**Negative**
I/We/You/They **have** ('ve) **left**. He/She/It **has** ('s) **left**.	I/We/You/They **have not** (haven't) **left**. He/She/It **has not** (hasn't) **left**.
Interrogative	**Short answers**
Have I/we/you/they **left**? **Has** he/she/it **left**?	Yes, I/we/you/they **have**./ No, I/we/you/they **haven't**. Yes, he/she/it **has**./ No, he/she/it **hasn't**.

We use the present perfect:
- **for actions which started in the past and continue up to the present.** *He **has lived** in Florida for five years.* (He started living in Florida five years ago and he still lives there.)
- **to refer to a personal experience.** *I **have visited** Mexico.* (When? We do not know.)

Time words/expressions used with the present perfect: *just, already, yet, for, since, never, ever, this week*, etc.

Note: *She **has gone** to Warsaw.* (She went to Warsaw and is still out there.)
*She **has been** to Warsaw.* (She went to Warsaw and returned. She is back now.)

2 Write the past participle of the verbs. Check in the dialogue.

1 swim ....
2 stay ....
3 visit ....
4 be ....
5 see ....
6 try ....
7 book ....
8 drive ....

3 Use the verbs in Ex. 2 in the present perfect to complete the sentences.

1 She *has seen* the studios. (✓)
2 Steve .... to Rabat. (✗)
3 They .... with dolphins. (✗)
4 Lisa .... Orlando once. (✓)
5 I .... couscous but I don't really like it. (✓)
6 Ken .... in this hotel.(✗)
7 I .... all the way from Arizona on my own. (✓)
8 We .... our tickets. (✗)

4 Put the verbs in brackets into the *present perfect interrogative*, then answer the questions.

1 A: *Have you ridden* **(you/ride)** an elephant before?
   B: Yes, *I have*.
2 A: .... **(they/fly)** in a helicopter?
   B: No, ...They're afraid of heights.
3 A: .... **(you/be)** on a boat trip before?
   B: No, ... It's my first time!
4 A: .... **(they/live)** in Mexico City for a long time?
   B: No, ...They moved there a month ago.
5 A: .... **(Bob/tell)** you the news?
   B: Yes, ... We're going to India!
6 A: .... **(Paula/sleep)** in a tent?
   B Yes, ... She loves camping.

Present perfect + *Ever/Never*

- We use **ever** in questions and statements.
  *Have you **ever** visited India? India is the best place I've **ever** visited.*
- We use **never** in statements.
  *I've **never** visited Poland. I haven't visited Poland.*

5 Ask and answer questions, as in the example.

Peru	Italy	Egypt	Spain
Australia	Poland	Brazil	Vietnam

A: *Peru is the best country I've **ever** visited. Have you **ever** been there?*

B: *No, I've **never** been there.*

Present perfect + *Yet/Already*

- We use **already** in questions and statements.
- We use **yet** in questions and negatives.
  - A: *Have you packed your suitcase **yet**?*
  - B: ***No**, I haven't. I haven't packed it **yet**. / **Yes**, I have. I've **already** packed it.*

6 🎧 *Kate and Ann are in Paris.* **Listen and tick (✓) what they have already done. In pairs, ask and answer questions, as in the example.**

1 visit the Eiffel Tower ✓
2 go to Versailles ☐
3 go shopping ☐
4 see the Arc de Triomphe ☐
5 go on a boat trip on the Seine ☐
6 visit the Louvre ☐
7 see Notre Dame ☐

A: *Have they visited the Eiffel Tower **yet**?*
B: *Yes, they have **already** visited the Eiffel Tower. Have they been to Versailles **yet**?*
A: *No, they haven't been to Versailles **yet**.*

Present perfect + *Just*

We use **just** in statements to show that an action finished only a few minutes earlier.
  - A: *Have you packed your suitcase yet?*
  - B: *Yes, I've **just** packed it.*

7 👥 **Read the theory. Ask and answer questions, as in the example.**

1 book a table
2 order lunch
3 speak to the receptionist
4 meet the guide

A: *Have you booked a table **yet**?*
B: *Yes, I've **just** booked it.*

Present perfect + *For/Since*

- We use **for** to express duration.
  - *I've been here **for** five days.*
- We use **since** to state a starting point.
  - *I've been here **since** Monday.*

8 **Write sentences. Use: *for* or *since*.**

1 He/be in Cairo/Friday
   *He has been in Cairo **since** Friday.*
2 He/live in Rome/three years
3 I/not see/Jane/ten years
4 I/not travel/by train/2015
5 They/be/on holiday/last Monday

9 **Put the verbs in brackets into the *present perfect* or the *past simple*.**

Hi Tracy,

Greetings from San Juan, Puerto Rico. I'm sorry I **1)** .... **(not/write)** for so long. We **2)** .... **(arrive)** here a week ago and I **3)** .... **(be)** busy exploring the place. It's one of the best islands I **4)** .... **(ever/visit)**. I **5)** .... **(cycle)** around most of the island so far. I **6)** .... **(already/swim)** at most of the beaches here and I **7)** .... **(try)** scuba diving! It **8)** .... **(be)** amazing. I **9)** .... **(not/buy)** any souvenirs yet, but there is plenty of time for that.

Yesterday, we **10)** .... **(go)** to the underground caves of Río Camuy Cave Park. We **11)** .... **(never/see)** such a beautiful place! Talk soon,

Anna

The

- We use **the** with the names of: rivers *(the Nile)*, oceans *(the Atlantic Ocean)*, seas *(the Baltic Sea)*, deserts *(the Sahara Desert)*, unique landmarks *(the Eiffel Tower)*, hotels *(the Royal)*, museums *(the British Museum)*, mountain ranges *(the Alps)*, groups of islands *(the Maldives)*.
- We don't use **the** with the names of: countries *(Egypt)*, cities *(London)*, streets *(Oxford Street)*, parks *(Hyde Park)*, single mountains *(Everest)*, lakes *(Lake Como)*, single islands *(Malta)*, continents *(Asia)*.

10 **Read the theory. Fill in *the* where necessary.**

1 Have you ever climbed .... Mont Blanc in .... Alps?
2 They go to .... Canary Islands every year.
3 I haven't been to .... New York before.
4 The museum in .... Baker Street is open now.
5 We're staying at .... Blue Hotel for five nights.
6 .... Pacific Ocean is the largest ocean in the world.
7 .... Taj Mahal is in .... Agra, India.
8 .... Lake Victoria is the largest lake in .... Africa.

11 〈THINK〉 👥 **Ask your partner questions. Use the present perfect. Your partner answers them.**

A: *Have you ever been to Egypt?*
B: *No, I haven't. Not yet.*

Skills in Action

Vocabulary

Travel experiences

1 Look at the pictures. In pairs, ask and answer, as in the example. You can use these adjectives: *exciting, fantastic, amazing, great, terrible, difficult.*

go on a helicopter tour

go ice skating

go camping

go snorkelling

go canoeing

swim with dolphins

A: Have you ever been on a helicopter tour?
B: Yes, I have. It was amazing./No, I haven't.

Listening

2 Listen to three short telephone conversations. For each question, choose the correct answer.

1 What has Sally done so far?
  A gone ice skating   **C** gone canoeing
  B gone on a helicopter tour

2 When did John arrive in New Zealand?
  A three days ago   **C** yesterday
  B last week

3 Ben is calling Kevin to ...
  A ask him to go on holiday together.
  B invite him to his house.
  C tell him about his holiday.

Everyday English

Describing a holiday experience

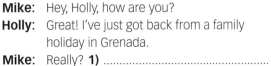

3 a) Complete the dialogue with the phrases A-E.

Mike: Hey, Holly, how are you?
Holly: Great! I've just got back from a family holiday in Grenada.
Mike: Really? **1)** ....
Holly: We went two weeks ago and got back this morning.
Mike: **2)** ....
Holly: Oh, it was wonderful! I had the time of my life!
Mike: Nice. **3)** ....
Holly: We went snorkelling at the Underwater Sculpture Park. There were beautiful statues at the bottom of the sea!
Mike: Wow! **4)** ....
Holly: We also visited the National Museum and Annandale Falls. I've taken lots of photos.
Mike: It sounds amazing.
Holly: It was. **5)** ....

A What did you do there?
B I can't wait to go again!
C When did you go?
D What was it like there?
E What else did you do?

b) Listen and check.

4 You have just come back from your holidays. Use phrases from the useful language box to act out a dialogue similar to the one in Ex. 3a.

Asking about holidays	Describing holidays
• When did you go? • How was it? • Was there much to do there? • What things could you do there? • Did you do anything else?	• We went last June/etc. • It was terrific! • I had an amazing/a lovely time! • There were amazing/ beautiful/fantastic ... • I also took/went on/visited ...

Pronunciation /h/ pronounced or silent

5 Listen and circle the words where *h* is silent. Listen again and repeat.

happy – hour – rhyme – hair – while – John – holiday – behind – school – how

Reading & Writing

6 Look at the blog entry and the blog comments below. What is the topic of the blog post? Read to find out.

William's Blog

Hi, everyone!
Some friends and I want to travel abroad this summer. We want to visit as many places as possible. Do you have any suggestions? Leave a comment below.

My Account:

Search

| About me | Photos | Contact |

Hi, William! Charlotte here. <u>Love your blog.</u>

I'm in Chile and I love it! So far, I've been camping and I've been canoeing. I've even been sandboarding in the Atacama Desert. It was a bit difficult and very hot – but it was fun! I had a great time. Go there – I'm sure you'll love it. <u>Can't wait for your next post!</u>

Posted 16/06

Hey, this is Jamie.

For me, Japan is the perfect place to go. I've visited the Ryukyu Islands many times and I've always had an amazing time there. Last time, I went windsurfing at Tebiro Beach. I also visited the medieval castle of Shuri and went hiking in the forests. I had the time of my life. Check out some of the photos I've taken. <u>By the way, great blog William.</u> <u>Looking forward to your next post!</u>

Posted 17/06

7 Read the blog comments again and make notes in the table.

	Place	Activities	Feelings
Charlotte	*Chile*		
Jamie			

Writing Tip

Writing a blog comment
When we read a blog entry, we can respond and write a **blog comment**. When we write a blog comment, we use **informal language**.
We start our blog comment by **greeting** the blogger (*Hey, Nick!*) and **introducing** ourselves. (*Tina from the UK here.*) Then we write our comment.
We end our comment with **closing remarks**. (*Can't wait for your next post!*)
We can also make a general comment about the blog entry either at the beginning or the end. (*Love your blog!*)

8 Read the *Writing Tip* box. Replace the underlined phrases in the blog comments in Ex. 6 with the ones below.

- Can't wait to read your next post!
- I really enjoy reading your blog.
- Great blog!
- Post again soon!

Writing (a blog comment about a holiday experience)

9 Think of a place you have been to. Make notes under the headings: *name – activities – feelings*.

10 Use your notes from Ex. 9 to write your blog comment on William's blog recommending a place to go (60-80 words). Follow the plan.

Plan
- greet blogger, introduce yourself
- write your comments (where you have been, what you have done there, your feelings)
- recommendation, closing remarks

VALUES

Acceptance
Culture makes people understand each other better.
(Paulo Coehlo)

 VIDEO

Adventure
Holidays

Do you want an exciting holiday experience? Then look no further! Wild Canadian Adventure Holidays promises the perfect holiday for you.

Package holidays on offer this month

A

From $1200 per person for 5 days

British Columbia

Imagine canoeing through the Rocky Mountains and sailing around Vancouver Island. Book one of our British Columbia package holidays and make your dream come true. We also offer trips to northern British Columbia where you can go camping, see Native American totem poles and even watch the beautiful Northern Lights in the night sky.

BOOK ONLINE NOW

B

Ontario

Have you ever wanted to go on a helicopter tour over a big city? Then Toronto with its amazing tall buildings is the place to go! Nature lovers can go on a boat ride around Niagara Falls. In winter, you can also go ice skating on the many frozen lakes around Ontario.

From $800 per person for 5 days

BOOK ONLINE NOW

Listening & Reading

1 Go through the text quickly. What is it about? Which place can you go camping? How can you see Niagara Falls?

2 🎧 Read or listen to the text. In which place (A or B):

1 can you see a city from the air?
2 is there a special evening attraction?
3 can you stay in a tent?
4 can you do a winter sport?

✅ **Check these words**

package holiday, trip, nature lover, frozen

Speaking & Writing

3 THINK Can you think of a dream holiday destination? How would you start the description to make people want to visit?

4 ICT 💬 Design a travel brochure for tourist destinations in your country. Write about exciting things visitors can see and/or do there.

Vocabulary

1 Fill in: *see, visit, go (x2), try, buy, take, ride.*

1 You can .... cheap souvenirs here.
2 You should .... the market in the Old City.
3 Don't forget to .... photos of your trip.
4 I want to .... all the local dishes.
5 Let's .... on a day trip to Casablanca.
6 We went to Fez to .... ancient buildings.
7 I had a chance to .... a camel in Egypt.
8 Tim didn't want to .... sightseeing.

(8 X 2 = 16)

2 Match to form collocations.

1	☐ helicopter	A	holidays
2	☐ frozen	B	skating
3	☐ traditional	C	souvenirs
4	☐ summer	D	tour
5	☐ handmade	E	restaurant
6	☐ ice	F	market
7	☐ noisy	G	lake

(7 X 2 = 14)

Grammar

3 Correct the mistakes.

1 "Has John finished his homework?" "No, he **has**."
2 The children **didn't** tried canoeing before.
3 "Where's Ida?" "She's **been** to the supermarket."
4 My uncle **have** lived in the same street all his life.
5 "Have you seen Jim?" "Yes, I **haven't**."
6 I have **gone** to Paris three times.

(6 X 2 = 12)

4 Fill in: *just, yet, since, for, never, ever, already.*

1 You don't need to book the hotel. Tim's ....
done it.
2 The plane has .... landed.
3 Lynn has lived here .... 2007.
4 Pat has .... ridden an elephant. It's his first time.
5 Monica has worked at the museum .... five
years.
6 Have you .... visited Rome?
7 They haven't come back from the safari ....

(7 X 2 = 14)

5 Put the verbs in brackets into the *present perfect* or the *past simple.*

Hi, Matt!

Greetings from London! I'm staying here with my uncle. We **1)** .... (already/visit) Buckingham Palace. We **2)** .... (go) there on Friday. My uncle also **3)** .... (take) me to Oxford Street yesterday, but I **4)** .... (not/buy) anything there. There are a lot of things I **5)** .... (not/do) yet. We **6)** .... (not/be) to Madame Tussauds yet and we **7)** .... (not/ride) in a London taxi. I really want to do that! What about you? **8)** .... (you/have) an exciting summer so far?

See you soon.

Greg

(8 X 3 = 24)

Everyday English

6 Match the exchanges.

1	☐ When did you go to Scotland?	A	We also visited a museum.
2	☐ How was it?	B	It was. I can't wait to go again.
3	☐ What did you do?	C	Last weekend.
4	☐ Did you do anything else?	D	We went canoeing.
5	☐ It sounds great.	E	It was terrific!

(5 X 4 = 20)
Total 100

Competences

GOOD ✓

VERY GOOD ✓ ✓

EXCELLENT ✓ ✓ ✓

Lexical Competence
Talk about
• holiday activities
• travel experiences

Reading Competence
• read for specific information (T/F statements; multiple matching)

Listening Competence
• listen for specific information (multiple choice)

Speaking Competence
• describe a holiday experience

Writing Competence
• write a blog comment about a holiday experience

Values: Environmental awareness

▶ VIDEO

Green Cities

A lot of cities nowadays are full of traffic, rubbish and air pollution. To stop this, cities must 'go green'! Here is how:

Create more **parks**. Parks are the lungs of a city. They give clean air to cities and are a relaxing place for people to spend their free time.

Create **public spaces**, such as pedestrian-only streets. They encourage people to get around on foot. There is less pollution from cars.

Encourage people to use **public transport** such as buses and trains. They can also use **cycle lanes** to move around quickly. All this means less traffic.

Set up **recycling programmes** for all kinds of waste like cans, bottles and electronics. This way, there is less rubbish.

Use **clean energy**, such as solar power and wind power. This way, we can have clean air and save money.

Perhaps it's challenging to go green. But when we do these simple things, we make cities better places to work, play and live our lives.

1 How can a city 'go green'?
🎧 Listen and read to find out.

2 Read the text again. Then, copy and complete the table in your notebook.

Suggestions	Benefits
Parks	*clean air, relaxing place for people*

3 THINK 👥 How green is the place where you live? Does it have any of the characteristics in the text? Discuss with your partner.

4 ICT 💬 Collect information about more characteristics of a green city and prepare a leaflet.

Public Speaking Skills

1 **a)** **Read the task.**

> Imagine you're at a local Earth Day event. You're the environmental club's representative. Present an example of a green city to the audience.

b) 🎧 **Listen and read the model. Put the slides into the correct order. Which slide is not very effective? Why?**

A ☐ **Cycle Lanes**

B ☐ **Recycling Programmes**

C ☐ **Parks**

D ☐ **Life in a big city**

Big cities have got dirty streets, tall overcrowded buildings and air pollution.

E ☐ **Singapore – A green city**

Hello, I'm Saanvi Lim. Dirty streets ... tall buildings ... air pollution. That's life in a big city, right? Well, in my city, Singapore in Asia, we all work hard to create a greener, healthier environment.

Let's take a look at some of the things we do. First, there are over 300 parks and gardens, and four nature reserves. These are home to rare plants and animals, and they provide the city with fresh, clean air. Educational tours of the parks also help people learn about the environment. Cycling is now the main mode of transport in Singapore. A 150-kilometre network of cycle lanes connects all the parks and there are cycle lanes in business and shopping areas, too. This means less traffic and air pollution, and people are healthier because they get more exercise. Thirdly, there are special programmes to encourage people and companies to recycle. There are recycling bins in public areas and outside houses. A lot of factories also take back e-waste for recycling and schools recycle their food waste. This way, we have less rubbish.

Singapore's nickname is the City in a Garden and I think it's a great name for such a green place! What if every city follows its example? Are there any questions? ... Thank you for listening.

2 **a)** **ICT Collect information about a green city in your country or another country. Make notes under the headings:** *Name/Location of city – Characteristics – How people help the environment*.

b) **Use your notes to prepare slides and give a digital presentation.**

CLIL: Citizenship

Living in the World Today

We are all citizens of the world.
So, it is important that we all know how to live in it!
To be a good citizen of the world, it is a good idea to ...

1

help other people.

2

be **polite** and not be a bully.

3

THINK OUTSIDE THE BOX

be **creative**.

4

listen to **everyone's opinion**.

5

care for **nature**.

6

keep **learning** about the world around you.

Listening & Reading

1 Look at the leaflet. How can we be good citizens of the world today?
🎧 Listen and read to find out.

2 Match the examples (A-F) to the tips (1-6) on how to be a good citizen.

We can ...

A ☐ make new friends.

B ☐ care for a grandparent.

C ☐ read lots of books.

D ☐ help plant trees.

E ☐ try to come up with new ideas.

F ☐ ask others what they think.

Speaking & Writing

3 (THINK) What else do you think you can do to be a good citizen?

4 💬 PROJECT Find photos which show what makes someone a good citizen. Design your own poster about how to be a good citizen of the world.

CLIL: Geography

CLIMATE ZONES

*A country's **climate** is what its weather is like over a long period of time. Countries in different parts of the world have different climates. There are 12 different types of climate worldwide and three main climate zones: **polar**, **temperate** and **tropical**.*

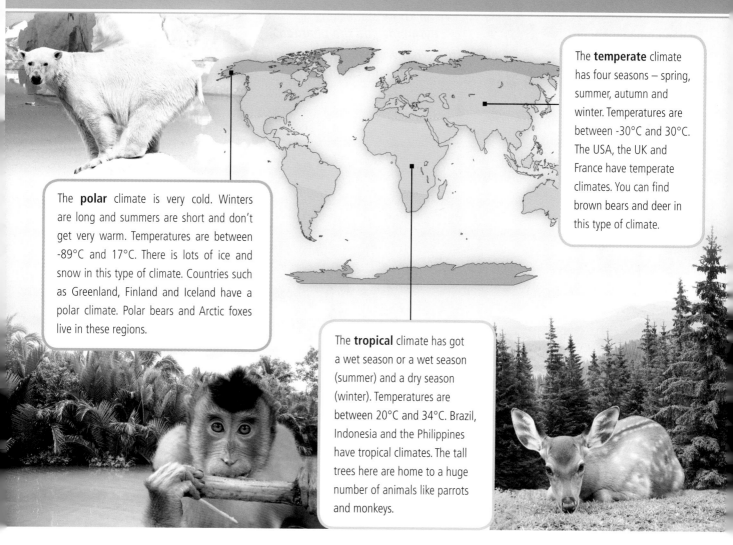

The **temperate** climate has four seasons – spring, summer, autumn and winter. Temperatures are between -30°C and 30°C. The USA, the UK and France have temperate climates. You can find brown bears and deer in this type of climate.

The **polar** climate is very cold. Winters are long and summers are short and don't get very warm. Temperatures are between -89°C and 17°C. There is lots of ice and snow in this type of climate. Countries such as Greenland, Finland and Iceland have a polar climate. Polar bears and Arctic foxes live in these regions.

The **tropical** climate has got a wet season or a wet season (summer) and a dry season (winter). Temperatures are between 20°C and 34°C. Brazil, Indonesia and the Philippines have tropical climates. The tall trees here are home to a huge number of animals like parrots and monkeys.

Listening & Reading

1 How many main climate zones are there? How many seasons has each got? 🎧 Listen and read to find out.

Speaking & Writing

2 Read again. Then, copy and complete the table in your notebook. Use your notes to compare the different types of climates. Tell the class.

Climate	Polar	Temperate	Tropical
Weather/Seasons			
Temperatures			
Countries			
Animals			

3 **ICT** Collect information about the climate in your country and another country. Write a short text comparing and contrasting the climates of the two countries.

109

CLIL: History

EVERYDAY LIFE IN ANCIENT
EGYPT

We all know something about the Pyramids and the pharaohs, but what was life like for ordinary ancient Egyptians?

Jobs

Most people were farmers. They had the River Nile for water, so it was usually easy to grow food. There were also many skilled workers, like builders, potters, weavers and painters.

Food

Bread was very **important** in the **diet**. There were vegetables like onions, cucumbers and beans, and fruit like figs and melons. They had chickens for eggs and cows for milk and cheese. Fish was often on the dinner table, another gift from the river.

Homes

Rich people had big stone houses with many rooms, but most people had small mud-brick houses. They were easy to make and quite **cool** in summer. Houses had **flat** roofs, so people could sit up there after **sunset**.

Travel

The Nile was the best way to travel. Boats were on the river day and night, with both goods and **passengers**.

Education

For most children, there was no school. Richer children had a general **education**, with lessons in hieroglyphics (the ancient Egyptian writing system) and mathematics.

Listening & Reading

1 Look at the pictures. Say three things you expect to read in the text.

🎧 Listen and read. Were your guesses correct?

2 Read the text again. Write *T* for True and *F* for False. Explain the words in bold.

1 Most people in ancient Egypt were painters. ....
2 The ancient Egyptians didn't eat fish. ....
3 Rich and poor people had the same houses. ....
4 All ancient Egyptian children had school lessons. ....
5 People could travel by water in ancient Egypt. ....

Speaking & Writing

3 THINK Compare life in ancient Egypt to your life. Say two things that are the same and two things that are different.

4 ICT 👥 Work in groups. Choose a time between 3000 BC and 30 BC in your country. Find out about everyday life and prepare a presentation. Use the headings: *jobs – food – education – homes – travel*.

H G Wells (1866-1946) was a British science-fiction writer. His famous book 'The Time Machine' tells the story of a man who travels through time into the future. There he meets the Eloi and the Morlocks, and makes friends with a girl called Weena.

THE TIME MACHINE

Weena quickly became my friend. One evening, as we walked through a beautiful garden with flowers and trees, we saw a strange-looking creature like an ape with red eyes. It ran across the grass and disappeared down a well.

"That was a Morlock" said Weena. "They live underground."

I knew then that this future world was not as good as I thought. I decided to follow the Morlock and climbed down the small, dark well. I lit a match and saw three Morlocks running away down a passage. They were afraid of the light. The passage led into a big underground room. I could hear machines and smell meat. Then the Morlocks saw me and started chasing me. I was scared. I ran back down the passage and climbed up into the garden.

"Why are they chasing me?" I asked Weena.

"They hunt the Eloi," she said. "It's dangerous here!"

We found somewhere to hide. Then she told me more. A long time ago, the Eloi were powerful. They made the Morlocks live underground. The Morlocks worked and served the Eloi. In their dark home, the Morlocks began to hate the daylight and the Eloi. Soon, they felt it was time to take power and make the Eloi afraid of them …

> ✓ **Check these words**
>
> ape, disappear, well, underground, passage, powerful, daylight

Listening & Reading

1 Who was H G Wells? What type of stories did he write? Read the biography to find out.

2 Look at the picture in the text. Who is in it? Where are they?
🎧 Listen and read to find out.

3 Read the extract and for questions 1-3 choose the correct answer (*A, B* or *C*).

1 The Time Traveller realised that the future world
   A was better than the past one.
   B had some problems.
   C was too strange to live in.

2 What are the Morlocks scared of?
   A the Time Traveller
   B the noisy machines
   C the bright light

3 Why did the Morlocks begin to live underground?
   A The Eloi sent them there.
   B They wanted to get more power.
   C They didn't like the daylight.

Speaking & Writing

4 (THINK) Do you feel sorry for the Morlocks? Why (not)?

5 **ICT** Find another story by H. G. Wells. Present it to the class. Say who the main characters are, where and when the story takes place and what happens in the story.

Word List

Unit 1 – Hi!

1a

amazing /əˈmeɪzɪŋ/ (adj)
American /əˈmerɪkən/ (adj)
Argentina /ˌɑːdʒənˈtiːnə/ (n)
Argentinian /ˌɑːdʒənˈtɪniən/ (adj)
become /bɪˈkʌm/ (v)
Brazil /brəˈzɪl/ (n)
Brazilian /brəˈzɪliən/ (adj)
Canada /ˈkænədə/ (n)
Canadian /kəˈneɪdiən/ (adj)
cardinal number /ˌkɑːdɪnəl ˈnʌmbə/ (n)
crazy about /ˈkreɪzi əbaʊt/ (adj)
design /dɪˈzaɪn/ (v)
draw /drɔː/ (v)
good at /ɡʊd ət/ (adj)
Greece /ɡriːs/ (n)
Greek /ɡriːk/ (adj)
interested in /ˈɪntrəstɪd ˈɪn/ (adj)
Japan /dʒəˈpæn/ (n)
Japanese /ˌdʒæpəˈniːz/ (adj)
mad about /ˈmæd əbaʊt/ (adj)
Mexican /ˈmeksɪkən/ (adj)
Mexico /ˈmeksɪkəʊ/ (n)
nationality /ˌnæʃəˈnæləti/ (n)
outfit /ˈaʊtfɪt/ (n)
snapshot /ˈsnæpʃɒt/ (n)
social media profile /ˌsəʊʃəl ˈmiːdiə ˌprəʊfaɪl/ (n)
Spain /speɪn/ (n)
Spanish /ˈspænɪʃ/ (adj)
the USA /ðə ˌjuː es ˈeɪ/ (n)
Turkey /ˈtɜːki/ (n)
Turkish /ˈtɜːkɪʃ/ (adj)

1b

actor /ˈæktə/ (n)
actress /ˈæktrəs/ (n)
architect /ˈɑːkɪtekt/ (n)
artist /ˈɑːtɪst/ (n)
astronaut /ˈæstrənɔːt/ (n)
cook /kʊk/ (v)
dance /dɑːns/ (v)
doctor /ˈdɒktə/ (n)
e-friend /ˈiː frend/ (n)
engineer /ˌendʒɪˈnɪə/ (n)
fast /fɑːst/ (adv)
pilot /ˈpaɪlət/ (n)
play the guitar (phr)
police officer /pəˈliːs ˌɒfɪsə/ (n)
run /rʌn/ (v)
secretary /ˈsekrətəri/ (n)
swim /swɪm/ (v)
type /taɪp/ (v)
vet /vet/ (n)
waiter /ˈweɪtə/ (n)

waitress /ˈweɪtrəs/ (n)
well /wel/ (adv)

1c

ability /əˈbɪləti/ (n)
Art /ɑːt/ (n)
Biology /baɪˈɒlədʒi/ (n)
Chemistry /ˈkemɪstri/ (n)
Computer Science /kəmˌpjuːtə ˈsaɪəns/ (n)
create /kriˈeɪt/ (v)
Drama /ˈdrɑːmə/ (n)
English Language /ˌɪŋglɪʃ ˈlæŋgwɪdʒ/ (n)
Geography /dʒiˈɒɡrəfi/ (n)
greeting /ˈɡriːtɪŋ/ (n)
History /ˈhɪstəri/ (n)
How are you? (phr)
How old are you? (phr)
How's everything? (phr)
I'm OK. (phr)
intonation /ˌɪntəˈneɪʃən/ (n)
introduction /ˌɪntrəˈdʌkʃən/ (n)
join /dʒɔɪn/ (v)
link /lɪŋk/ (v)
Literature /ˈlɪtrətʃə/ (n)
Maths /mæθs/ (n)
Music /ˈmjuːzɪk/ (n)
Nice to meet you! (phr)
Not bad. (phr)
opposing /əˈpəʊzɪŋ/ (adj)
personal /ˈpɜːsənəl/ (adj)
Physics /ˈfɪzɪks/ (n)
Pleased to meet you! (phr)
See you! (phr)
similar /ˈsɪmələ/ (adj)
so-so /ˈsəʊ səʊ/ (adv)
sportsman /ˈspɔːtsmən/ (n)
student /ˈstjuːdənt/ (n)
study /ˈstʌdi/ (v)
too /tuː/ (adv)
web page /ˈweb peɪdʒ/ (n)
What's your job? (phr)
What's your name? (phr)
Where are you from? (phr)

Culture 1

black /blæk/ (adj)
blue /bluː/ (adj)
brown /braʊn/ (adj)
capital /ˈkæpɪtl/ (n)
coat of arms /ˌkəʊt əv ˈɑːmz/ (n)
colour guide /ˈkʌlə gaɪd/ (n)
continent /ˈkɒntɪnənt/ (n)
currency /ˈkʌrənsi/ (n)
dollar /ˈdɒlə/ (n)

English-speaking /ˌɪŋglɪʃ ˌspiːkɪŋ/ (adj)
euro /ˈjʊərəʊ/ (n)
flag /flæg/ (n)
green /griːn/ (adj)
grey /greɪ/ (adj)
native speaker /ˌneɪtɪv ˈspiːkə/ (n)
nearly /ˈnɪəli/ (adv)
official language /əˌfɪʃəl ˈlæŋgwɪdʒ/ (n)
orange /ˈɒrɪndʒ/ (adj)
pink /pɪŋk/ (adj)
population /ˌpɒpjəˈleɪʃən/ (n)
pound /paʊnd/ (n)
purple /ˈpɜːpəl/ (adj)
red /red/ (adj)
same /seɪm/ (adj)
white /waɪt/ (adj)
yellow /ˈjeləʊ/ (adj)

Unit 2 – Families

2a

appearance /əˈpɪərəns/ (n)
aunt /ɑːnt/ (n)
bald /bɔːld/ (adj)
billionaire /ˌbɪljəˈneə/ (n)
brother /ˈbrʌðə/ (n)
cheek /tʃiːk/ (n)
chin /tʃɪn/ (n)
cousin /ˈkʌzən/ (n)
cry /kraɪ/ (v)
curly /ˈkɜːli/ (adj)
dark /dɑːk/ (adj)
daughter /ˈdɔːtə/ (n)
fair /feə/ (adj)
family /ˈfæməli/ (n)
family tree /ˈfæməli triː/ (n)
father /ˈfɑːðə/ (n)
full /fʊl/ (adj)
gardening /ˈɡɑːdnɪŋ/ (n)
granddad /ˈɡrændæd/ (n)
granddaughter /ˈɡrænˌdɔːtə/ (n)
grandfather /ˈɡrændˌfɑːðə/ (n)
grandma /ˈɡrænmɑː/ (n)
grandmother /ˈɡrænˌmʌðə/ (n)
grandparent /ˈɡrænˌpeərənt/ (n)
husband /ˈhʌzbənd/ (n)
imagine /ɪˈmædʒɪn/ (v)
juggle /ˈdʒʌgəl/ (v)
laugh /lɑːf/ (v)
lip /lɪp/ (n)
long /lɒŋ/ (adj)
look after /ˈlʊk ɑːftə/ (phr v)
look like (phr)
middle-aged /ˌmɪdl ˈeɪdʒd/ (adj)
mother /ˈmʌðə/ (n)

moustache /məˈstɑːʃ/ (n)
mouth /maʊθ/ (n)
naughty /ˈnɔːti/ (adj)
nephew /ˈnefjuː/ (n)
normal /ˈnɔːməl/ (adj)
nose /nəʊz/ (n)
octopus /ˈɒktəpəs/ (n)
old /əʊld/ (adj)
parent /ˈpeərənt/ (n)
plump /plʌmp/ (adj)
serious /ˈsɪəriəs/ (adj)
short /ʃɔːt/ (adj)
sister /ˈsɪstə/ (n)
slim /slɪm/ (adj)
son /sʌn/ (n)
spider /ˈspaɪdə/ (n)
straight /streɪt/ (adj)
tall /tɔːl/ (adj)
tango /ˈtæŋgəʊ/ (n)
uncle /ˈʌŋkəl/ (n)
well-built /ˌwel ˈbɪlt/ (adj)
young /jʌŋ/ (adj)

2b

a bit /ə ˈbɪt/ (adv)
artist /ˈɑːtɪst/ (n)
beach /biːtʃ/ (n)
beard /bɪəd/ (n)
blonde /blɒnd/ (adj)
brush /brʌʃ/ (n)
cool /kuːl/ (adj)
create /kriˈeɪt/ (v)
deer /dɪə/ (n)
different /ˈdɪfərənt/ (adj)
each other (phr)
glasses /ˈglɑːsɪz/ (pl n)
goldfish /ˈgəʊldfɪʃ/ (n)
hobby /ˈhɒbi/ (n)
knife /naɪf/ (n)
leaf /liːf/ (n)
match /mætʃ/ (n)
meet /miːt/ (v)
ox /ɒks/ (n)
personality /ˌpɜːsəˈnæləti/ (n)
sheep /ʃiːp/ (n)
smartphone /ˈsmɑːtfəʊn/ (n)
status /ˈsteɪtəs/ (n)
teacher /ˈtiːtʃə/ (n)
university /ˌjuːnɪˈvɜːsəti/ (n)
vet /vet/ (n)
wavy /ˈweɪvi/ (adj)

2c

actor /ˈæktə/ (n)
actress /ˈæktrəs/ (n)
blog entry /ˈblɒg entri/ (n)
brave /breɪv/ (adj)

clever /ˈklevə/ (adj)
close /kləʊs/ (adj)
famous /ˈfeɪməs/ (adj)
fond /fɒnd/ (adj)
funny /ˈfʌni/ (adj)
half-brother /ˈhɑːf brʌðə/ (n)
half-sister /ˈhɑːf sɪstə/ (n)
hard-working /ˌhɑːd ˈwɜːkɪŋ/ (adj)
impolite /ˌɪmpəˈlaɪt/ (adj)
kind /kaɪnd/ (adj)
lazy /ˈleɪzi/ (adj)
Lord /lɔːd/ (n)
manager /ˈmænɪdʒə/ (n)
noisy /ˈnɔɪzi/ (adj)
outgoing /ˈaʊtɡəʊɪŋ/ (adj)
poet /ˈpəʊɪt/ (n)
quiet /ˈkwaɪət/ (adj)
role /rəʊl/ (n)
series /ˈsɪəriːz/ (n)
serious /ˈsɪəriəs/ (adj)
shy /ʃaɪ/ (adj)
silly /ˈsɪli/ (adj)
smile /smaɪl/ (n)
What's he like? (phr)
wife /waɪf/ (n)
writer /ˈraɪtə/ (n)

Culture 2

businessman /ˈbɪznəsmæn/ (n)
by your side (phr)
celebrity /səˈlebrəti/ (n)
company /ˈkʌmpəni/ (n)
ex-coach /ˈeks kəʊtʃ/ (n)
fashion /ˈfæʃən/ (n)
hard-working /ˌhɑːd ˈwɜːkɪŋ/ (adj)
proud /praʊd/ (adj)
sibling /ˈsɪblɪŋ/ (n)
talented /ˈtæləntɪd/ (adj)
tennis player /ˈtenɪs pleɪə/ (n)
writer /ˈraɪtə/ (n)

Unit 3 – Home sweet home!
3a

appliance /əˈplaɪəns/ (n)
armchair /ˈɑːmtʃeə/ (n)
attic /ˈætɪk/ (n)
bath /bɑːθ/ (n)
bedside cabinet /bedsaɪd ˈkæbɪnət/ (n)
bookcase /ˈbʊkkeɪs/ (n)
cave house /ˈkeɪv haʊs/ (n)
chimney /ˈtʃɪmni/ (n)
cooker /ˈkʊkə/ (n)

cool /kuːl/ (adj)
cosy /ˈkəʊzi/ (adj)
cupboard /ˈkʌbəd/ (n)
curtain /ˈkɜːtən/ (n)
decoration /ˌdekəˈreɪʃən/ (n)
dining room /ˈdaɪnɪŋ ruːm/ (n)
double bed /ˌdʌbl ˈbed/ (n)
downstairs /ˌdaʊnˈsteəz/ (adv)
environment /ɪnˈvaɪrənmənt/ (n)
fridge /frɪdʒ/ (n)
furniture /ˈfɜːnɪtʃə/ (n)
garage /ˈɡærɪdʒ/ (n)
ground /ɡraʊnd/ (n)
ground floor /ˌɡraʊnd ˈflɔː/ (n)
hill /hɪl/ (n)
Home sweet home! (phr)
huge /hjuːdʒ/ (adj)
kitchen /ˈkɪtʃən/ (n)
large /lɑːdʒ/ (adj)
living room /ˈlɪvɪŋ ruːm/ (n)
main bedroom /ˌmeɪn ˈbedrʊm/ (n)
mirror /ˈmɪrə/ (n)
outside /aʊtˈsaɪd/ (prep)
pillow /ˈpɪləʊ/ (n)
pretty /ˈprɪti/ (adj)
roof /ruːf/ (n)
rug /rʌɡ/ (n)
save /seɪv/ (v)
single bed /ˌsɪŋɡl ˈbed/ (n)
sink /sɪŋk/ (n)
sofa /ˈsəʊfə/ (n)
spacious /ˈspeɪʃəs/ (adj)
stairs /steəz/ (pl n)
study room /ˈstʌdi ruːm/ (n)
toilet /ˈtɔɪlət/ (n)
towel /ˈtaʊəl/ (n)
underground /ˌʌndəˈɡraʊnd/ (adv)
unique /juːˈniːk/ (adj)
upstairs /ˌʌpˈsteəz/ (adv)
view /vjuː/ (n)
wall /wɔːl/ (n)
wardrobe /ˈwɔːdrəʊb/ (n)
warm /wɔːm/ (adj)
washbasin /ˈwɒʃˌbeɪsən/ (n)
wonderful /ˈwʌndəfəl/ (adj)
wooden /ˈwʊdn/ (adj)

3b

advert /ˈædvɜːt/ (n)
basement /ˈbeɪsmənt/ (n)
bookcase /ˈbʊkkeɪs/ (n)
contact /ˈkɒntækt/ (v)
cushion /ˈkʊʃən/ (n)
design /dɪˈzaɪn/ (v)

fireplace /ˈfaɪəpleɪs/ (n)
for rent (phr)
for sale (phr)
lamp /læmp/ (n)
painting /ˈpeɪntɪŋ/ (n)
poster /ˈpəʊstə/ (n)

3c

address /əˈdres/ (n)
available /əˈveɪləbəl/ (adj)
block of flats /ˌblɒk əv ˈflæts/ (n)
can't wait (phr)
comfortable /ˈkʌmftəbəl/ (adj)
cost /kɒst/ (n)
detached /dɪˈtætʃt/ (adj)
double /ˈdʌbəl/ (adj)
estate agent /ɪˈsteɪt eɪdʒənt/ (n)
feature /ˈfiːtʃə/ (n)
flat owner /ˈflæt ˌəʊnə/ (n)
heart /hɑːt/ (n)
information /ˌɪnfəˈmeɪʃən/ (n)
location /ləʊˈkeɪʃən/ (n)
rent /rent/ (v)
semi-detached /ˌsemi dɪˈtætʃt/ (adj)
terraced /ˈterəst/ (adj)
value /ˈvæljuː/ (n)

Culture 3

age /eɪdʒ/ (n)
amazing /əˈmeɪzɪŋ/ (adj)
building /ˈbɪldɪŋ/ (n)
centre /ˈsentə/ (n)
county /ˈkaʊnti/ (n)
garden /ˈɡɑːdən/ (n)
gatehouse /ˈɡeɪthaʊs/ (n)
head of state /ˌhed əv ˈsteɪt/ (n)
high /haɪ/ (adj)
impressive /ɪmˈpresɪv/ (adj)
inside /ɪnˈsaɪd/ (prep)
king /kɪŋ/ (n)
middle /ˈmɪdl/ (n)
monarch /ˈmɒnək/ (n)
monarchy /ˈmɒnəki/ (n)
office /ˈɒfɪs/ (n)
official /əˈfɪʃəl/ (adj)
open /ˈəʊpən/ (adj)
painting /ˈpeɪntɪŋ/ (n)
palace /ˈpæləs/ (n)
powerful /ˈpaʊəfəl/ (adj)
queen /kwiːn/ (n)
royal /ˈrɔɪəl/ (adj)
Royal Court /ˌrɔɪəl ˈkɔːt/ (n)
size /saɪz/ (n)
staff /stɑːf/ (n)
the front /ðə ˈfrʌnt/ (n)

the royal family /ðə ˌrɔɪəl ˈfæməli/ (n)
visit /ˈvɪzɪt/ (v)

Values A: National pride

courage /ˈkʌrɪdʒ/ (n)
different /ˈdɪfərənt/ (adj)
energy /ˈenədʒi/ (n)
flag /flæɡ/ (n)
freedom /ˈfriːdəm/ (n)
harmony /ˈhɑːməni/ (n)
honesty /ˈɒnəsti/ (n)
life /laɪf/ (n)
national /ˈnæʃənəl/ (adj)
nature /ˈneɪtʃə/ (n)
peace /piːs/ (n)
power /ˈpaʊə/ (n)
pride /praɪd/ (n)
shape /ʃeɪp/ (n)
strength /streŋθ/ (n)
stripe /straɪp/ (n)
symbol /ˈsɪmbəl/ (n)
value /ˈvæljuː/ (n)
wisdom /ˈwɪzdəm/ (n)

Public Speaking Skills

celebration /ˌseləˈbreɪʃən/ (n)
farmer /ˈfɑːmə/ (n)
humour /ˈhjuːmə/ (n)
meaning /ˈmiːnɪŋ/ (n)
point /pɔɪnt/ (n)
proud of /ˈpraʊd əv/ (adj)
public /ˈpʌblɪk/ (adj)
riddle /ˈrɪdl/ (n)
soldier /ˈsəʊldʒə/ (n)
special /ˈspeʃəl/ (adj)
student /ˈstjuːdənt/ (n)
trader /ˈtreɪdə/ (n)
worker /ˈwɜːkə/ (n)

Unit 4 – Busy days
4a

(a) quarter past (phr)
(a) quarter to (phr)
animal shelter /ˈænɪməl ˌʃeltə/ (n)
care for /ˈkeə fə/ (phr v)
catch the bus to college (phr)
chat with friends online (phr)
countryside /ˈkʌntrisaɪd/ (n)
daily routine /ˌdeɪli ruːˈtiːn/ (n)
do homework (phr)
finish college (phr)

113

Word List

get dressed (phr)
go back home (phr)
go jogging (phr)
go to bed (phr)
half past (phr)
have a break for lunch (phr)
have a shower (phr)
have breakfast (phr)
have dinner (phr)
in the afternoon (phr)
in the evening (phr)
in the morning (phr)
midday /ˌmɪd'deɪ/ (n)
o'clock /ə 'klɒk/ (adv)
satisfied /'sætɪsfaɪd/ (adj)
skype /skaɪp/ (v)
tell the time (phr)
tiring /'taɪərɪŋ/ (adj)
visitor /'vɪzɪtə/ (n)
wake up /ˌweɪk 'ʌp/ (phr v)
walk /wɔːk/ (n)
work part-time (phr)

4b

closed /kləʊzd/ (adj)
cook /kʊk/ (v)
cow /kaʊ/ (n)
do the washing-up (phr)
eat out /ˌiːt 'aʊt/ (phr v)
farmhouse /'fɑːmhaʊs/ (n)
feed /fiːd/ (v)
field /fiːld/ (n)
football practice /'fʊtbɔːl ˌpræktɪs/ (n)
frequency /'friːkwənsi/ (n)
go jogging (phr)
go out /ˌgəʊ 'aʊt/ (phr v)
go shopping (phr)
hospital /'hɒspɪtəl/ (n)
local /'ləʊkəl/ (adj)
milk /mɪlk/ (v)
playing field /'pleɪɪŋ fiːld/ (n)
refectory /rɪ'fektəri/ (n)
relax /rɪ'læks/ (v)
the open air /ðɪ ˌəʊpən 'eə/ (n)
though /ðəʊ/ (adv)

4c

art gallery /'ɑːt ˌgæləri/ (n)
cycle /'saɪkəl/ (v)
do yoga (phr)
free /friː/ (adj)
free-time activity /friː taɪm æk'tɪvəti/ (n)
fresh /freʃ/ (adj)
go dancing (phr)
go on a picnic (phr)

go snorkelling (phr)
go to the cinema (phr)
library /'laɪbrəri/ (n)
listen to music (phr)
make arrangements (phr)
market /'mɑːkɪt/ (n)
meet /miːt/ (v)
museum /mjuːˈziəm/ (n)
play /pleɪ/ (v)
read /riːd/ (v)
reason /'riːzən/ (n)
spend /spend/ (v)
visit /'vɪzɪt/ (v)
watch a film (phr)

Culture 4

annual /'ænjuəl/ (adj)
baseball /'beɪsbɔːl/ (n)
competition /ˌkɒmpə'tɪʃən/ (n)
cricket /'krɪkɪt/ (n)
curling /'kɜːlɪŋ/ (n)
enjoy /ɪn'dʒɔɪ/ (v)
ice hockey /'aɪs ˌhɒki/ (n)
lacrosse /lə'krɒs/ (n)
mad /mæd/ (adj)
official /ə'fɪʃəl/ (adj)
rugby /'rʌgbi/ (n)
skiing /'skiːɪŋ/ (n)
snowboarding /'snəʊbɔːdɪŋ/ (n)
surfing /'sɜːfɪŋ/ (n)
take part (phr)

Unit 5 – Birds of a Feather

5a

beak /biːk/ (n)
bear /beə/ (n)
claw /klɔː/ (n)
coast /kəʊst/ (n)
crocodile /'krɒkədaɪl/ (n)
dolphin /'dɒlfɪn/ (n)
eagle /'iːgəl/ (n)
easily /'iːzəli/ (adv)
elephant /'elɪfənt/ (n)
feather /'feðə/ (n)
feed on /'fiːd ɒn/ (v)
fin /fɪn/ (n)
flamingo /flə'mɪŋgəʊ/ (n)
friendly /'frendli/ (adj)
fur /fɜː/ (n)
giraffe /dʒə'rɑːf/ (n)
ice /aɪs/ (n)
intelligent /ɪn'telɪdʒənt/ (adj)
kayak tour /'kaɪæk tʊə/ (n)
lay eggs (phr)
lion /'laɪən/ (n)

mammal /'mæməl/ (n)
mane /meɪn/ (n)
monkey /'mʌŋki/ (n)
neck /nek/ (n)
offer /'ɒfə/ (v)
paw /pɔː/ (n)
penguin /'peŋgwɪn/ (n)
protect /prə'tekt/ (v)
reptile /'reptaɪl/ (n)
reserve /rɪ'zɜːv/ (n)
sharp /ʃɑːp/ (adj)
smile /smaɪl/ (n)
snake /sneɪk/ (n)
stripe /straɪp/ (n)
tail /teɪl/ (n)
thick /θɪk/ (adj)
tiger /'taɪgə/ (n)
trunk /trʌŋk/ (n)
unusual /ʌn'juːʒuəl/ (adj)
warm /wɔːm/ (adj)
weigh /weɪ/ (v)
welcome /'welkəm/ (v)
whisker /'wɪskə/ (n)
wild /waɪld/ (adj)
wing /wɪŋ/ (n)
zebra /'zebrə/ (n)

5b

acre /'eɪkə/ (n)
carry /'kæri/ (v)
continent /'kɒntɪnənt/ (n)
entrance fee /'entrəns fiː/ (n)
explore /ɪk'splɔː/ (v)
feed /fiːd/ (v)
grant a request (phr)
hide /haɪd/ (v)
pick up /ˌpɪk 'ʌp/ (phr v)
pouch /paʊtʃ/ (n)
preserve /prɪ'zɜːv/ (v)
species /'spiːʃiːz/ (n)
stripe /straɪp/ (n)
tank /tæŋk/ (n)
tongue /tʌŋ/ (n)
zookeeper /'zuːkiːpə/ (n)

5c

application form /ˌæplɪ'keɪʃən ˌfɔːm/ (n)
cow /kaʊ/ (n)
donkey /'dɒŋki/ (n)
duck /dʌk/ (n)
farm animal /'fɑːm ˌænɪməl/ (n)
goat /gəʊt/ (n)
goose /guːs/ (n)
hen /hen/ (n)
horse /hɔːs/ (n)

interested in /'ɪntrəstɪd ɪn/ (adj)
quite /kwaɪt/ (adv)
retired /rɪ'taɪəd/ (adj)
rooster /'ruːstə/ (n)
sheep /ʃiːp/ (n)
turkey /'tɜːki/ (n)
volunteer /ˌvɒlən'tɪə/ (v)

Culture 5

beaver /'biːvə/ (n)
bill /bɪl/ (n)
cute /kjuːt/ (adj)
eucalyptus /ˌjuːkə'lɪptəs/ (n)
fluffy /'flʌfi/ (adj)
ground /graʊnd/ (n)
home to /'həʊm tə/ (n)
hop /hɒp/ (v)
male /meɪl/ (adj)
otter /'ɒtə/ (n)
spoon /spuːn/ (n)
strange /streɪndʒ/ (adj)
unique /juː'niːk/ (adj)

Unit 6 – Come rain or shine

6a

ancient /'eɪnʃənt/ (adj)
blow /bləʊ/ (v)
cloudy /'klaʊdi/ (adj)
come rain or shine (idm)
dry /draɪ/ (adj)
fog /fɒg/ (n)
foggy /'fɒgi/ (adj)
freezing cold /ˌfriːzɪŋ 'kəʊld/ (adj)
golden /'gəʊldən/ (adj)
greetings /'griːtɪŋz/ (pl n)
in fact (phr)
rainy /'reɪni/ (adj)
sail /seɪl/ (v)
sand /sænd/ (n)
sightsee /'saɪtsiː/ (v)
snow /snəʊ/ (v)
snowy /'snəʊi/ (adj)
strange /streɪndʒ/ (adj)
sunny /'sʌni/ (adj)
temple /'tempəl/ (n)
warm /wɔːm/ (adj)
waterproof jacket /ˌwɔːtəpruːf 'dʒækɪt/ (n)
windy /'wɪndi/ (adj)

6b

ASAP (as soon as possible) (abbr)
barbecue /ˈbɑːbɪkjuː/ (n)
delicious /dɪˈlɪʃəs/ (adj)
gap year /ˈɡæp jɪə/ (n)
historic /hɪˈstɒrɪk/ (adj)
jog /dʒɒɡ/ (v)
monument /ˈmɒnjumənt/ (n)
pick sb up /ˌpɪk ˈʌp/ (phr v)
robotics /rəʊˈbɒtɪks/ (n)
sunbathe /ˈsʌnbeɪð/ (v)

6c

belt /belt/ (n)
blouse /blaʊz/ (n)
boot /buːt/ (n)
cap /kæp/ (n)
coat /kəʊt/ (n)
crowded /ˈkraʊdɪd/ (adj)
dress /dres/ (n)
glove /ɡlʌv/ (n)
guide /ɡaɪd/ (n)
hat /hæt/ (n)
high-heeled /ˌhaɪ hiːld/ (adj)
island /ˈaɪlənd/ (n)
item /ˈaɪtəm/ (n)
jacket /ˈdʒækɪt/ (n)
jeans /dʒiːnz/ (pl n)
medium /ˈmiːdiəm/ (adj)
postcode /ˈpəʊstkəʊd/ (n)
refund /rɪˈfʌnd/ (n)
sandal /ˈsændl/ (n)
scarf /skɑːf/ (n)
seaside /ˈsiːsaɪd/ (adj)
serve /sɜːv/ (v)
shirt /ʃɜːt/ (n)
shorts /ʃɔːts/ (pl n)
size /saɪz/ (n)
skirt /skɜːt/ (n)
sock /sɒk/ (n)
suit /suːt/ (n)
T-shirt /ˈtiː ʃɜːt/ (n)
tie /taɪ/ (n)
tight /taɪt/ (adj)
tights /taɪts/ (pl n)
top /tɒp/ (n)
trainers /ˈtreɪnəz/ (pl n)
trousers /ˈtraʊzəz/ (pl n)

Culture 6

desert /ˈdezət/ (n)
jumper /ˈdʒʌmpə/ (n)
pack /pæk/ (v)
protection /prəˈtekʃən/ (n)

Values B: Environmentalism

animal shelter /ˈænɪməl ˈʃeltə/ (n)
careful of /ˈkeəfl əv/ (adj)
carefully /ˈkeəfəli/ (adv)
change /tʃeɪndʒ/ (v)
choke on /ˈtʃəʊk ɒn/ (v)
driver /ˈdraɪvə/ (n)
entertain /ˌentəˈteɪn/ (v)
environmentalism /ɪnˌvaɪrənˈmentəlɪzəm/ (n)
far away (phr)
find out /ˌfaɪnd ˈaʊt/ (phr)
grow /ɡrəʊ/ (v)
hedgehog /ˈhedʒhɒɡ/ (n)
hit /hɪt/ (v)
in danger /ɪn ˈdeɪndʒə/ (prep phr)
inform /ɪnˈfɔːm/ (v)
insect /ˈɪnsekt/ (n)
interesting /ˈɪntrəstɪŋ/ (adj)
lid /lɪd/ (n)
look for /ˈlʊk fə/ (phr v)
mosquito /məˈskiːtəʊ/ (n)
need /niːd/ (v)
neighbourhood /ˈneɪbəhʊd/ (n)
persuade /pəˈsweɪd/ (v)
planet /ˈplænɪt/ (n)
plant /plɑːnt/ (n)
plant /plɑːnt/ (v)
poisoned /ˈpɔɪzənd/ (pp)
protect /prəˈtekt/ (v)
provide /prəˈvaɪd/ (v)
report /rɪˈpɔːt/ (v)
rubbish /ˈrʌbɪʃ/ (n)
rubbish bin /ˈrʌbɪʃ bɪn/ (n)
run a programme (phr)
shady /ˈʃeɪdi/ (adj)
start /stɑːt/ (v)
stray /streɪ/ (n)
watch out /ˌwɒtʃ ˈaʊt/ (phr v)

Public Speaking Skills

bright /braɪt/ (adv)
burn /bɜːn/ (v)
cut down /ˌkʌt ˈdaʊn/ (phr v)
description /dɪˈskrɪpʃən/ (n)
destroy /dɪˈstrɔɪ/ (v)
disappear /ˌdɪsəˈpɪə/ (v)
endangered /ɪnˈdeɪndʒəd/ (adj)
forest /ˈfɒrɪst/ (n)
grow /ɡrəʊ/ (v)
habit /ˈhæbɪt/ (n)
hunt /hʌnt/ (v)
hunter /ˈhʌntə/ (n)

lifespan /ˈlaɪfspæn/ (n)
pollution /pəˈluːʃən/ (n)
threat /θret/ (n)

Unit 7 – Taste the world

7a

apple pie /ˈæpəl paɪ/ (n)
beef /biːf/ (n)
biscuit /ˈbɪskɪt/ (n)
bowl /bəʊl/ (n)
bread /bred/ (n)
breakfast /ˈbrekfəst/ (n)
butter /ˈbʌtə/ (n)
cabbage /ˈkæbɪdʒ/ (n)
cereal /ˈsɪəriəl/ (n)
cheese /tʃiːz/ (n)
cherry /ˈtʃeri/ (n)
chicken /ˈtʃɪkɪn/ (n)
chocolate cake /ˈtʃɒklət keɪk/ (n)
choice /tʃɔɪs/ (n)
chopsticks /ˈtʃɒpstɪks/ (pl n)
coconut /ˈkəʊkənʌt/ (n)
crab /kræb/ (n)
cuisine /kwɪˈziːn/ (n)
culture /ˈkʌltʃə/ (n)
cutlery /ˈkʌtləri/ (n)
dairy /ˈdeəri/ (n)
dessert /dɪˈzɜːt/ (n)
dip /dɪp/ (v)
drink /drɪŋk/ (n)
fish /fɪʃ/ (n)
food /fuːd/ (n)
fork /fɔːk/ (n)
fruit /fruːt/ (n)
garlic /ˈɡɑːlɪk/ (n)
grain /ɡreɪn/ (n)
grape /ɡreɪp/ (n)
hungry /ˈhʌŋɡri/ (adj)
ice cream /ˌaɪs ˈkriːm/ (n)
ingredient /ɪnˈɡriːdiənt/ (n)
insulting /ɪnˈsʌltɪŋ/ (adj)
ketchup /ˈketʃəp/ (n)
knife /naɪf/ (n)
lamb /læm/ (n)
lettuce /ˈletɪs/ (n)
light /laɪt/ (adj)
meal /miːl/ (n)
meat /miːt/ (n)
milk /mɪlk/ (n)
mustard /ˈmʌstəd/ (n)
noodles /ˈnuːdlz/ (pl n)
onion /ˈʌnjən/ (n)
orange juice /ˈɒrəndʒ dʒuːs/ (n)
pancake /ˈpænkeɪk/ (n)
pasta /ˈpæstə/ (n)

pear /peə/ (n)
pepper /ˈpepə/ (n)
pineapple /ˈpaɪnæpəl/ (n)
plate /pleɪt/ (n)
poultry /ˈpəʊltri/ (n)
powder /ˈpaʊdə/ (n)
prawn /prɔːn/ (n)
refreshing /rɪˈfreʃɪŋ/ (adj)
rice /raɪs/ (n)
salad /ˈsæləd/ (n)
salt /sɔːlt/ (n)
salty /ˈsɔːlti/ (adj)
sauce /sɔːs/ (n)
seafood /ˈsiːfuːd/ (n)
seasoning /ˈsiːzənɪŋ/ (n)
speciality /speʃəliti/ (n)
spring roll /sprɪŋ ˈrəʊl/ (n)
strawberry /ˈstrɔːbəri/ (n)
sugar /ˈʃʊɡə/ (n)
sweet /swiːt/ (n)
tablespoon /ˈteɪbəlspuːn/ (n)
tableware /ˈteɪbəlweə/ (n)
taste /teɪst/ (v)
teaspoon /ˈtiːspuːn/ (n)
thirsty /ˈθɜːsti/ (adj)
tip /tɪp/ (n)
try /traɪ/ (v)
vegetable /ˈvedʒtəbəl/ (n)
weight /weɪt/ (n)

7b

bag /bæɡ/ (n)
bottle /ˈbɒtl/ (n)
burger /ˈbɜːɡə/ (n)
carton /ˈkɑːtn/ (n)
countable /ˈkaʊntəbəl/ (adj)
cucumber /ˈkjuːkʌmbə/ (n)
cup /kʌp/ (n)
eggplant /ˈeɡplɑːnt/ (n)
flour /ˈflaʊə/ (n)
glass /ɡlɑːs/ (n)
honey /ˈhʌni/ (n)
jam /dʒæm/ (n)
kilo /ˈkiːləʊ/ (n)
loaf /ləʊf/ (n)
olive oil /ˌɒlɪv ˈɔɪl/ (n)
packet /ˈpækɪt/ (n)
peach /piːtʃ/ (n)
piece /piːs/ (n)
pot /pɒt/ (n)
rainbow /ˈreɪnbəʊ/ (n)
sleepover /ˈsliːpəʊvə/ (n)
slice /slaɪs/ (n)
smoothie /ˈsmuːði/ (n)
uncountable /ʌnˈkaʊntəbəl/ (adj)
yoghurt /ˈjɒɡət/ (n)

Word List

7c

bake /beɪk/ (v)
baked potato /ˌbeɪkt pəˈteɪtəʊ/ (n)
boil /bɔɪl/ (v)
book /bʊk/ (v)
bottled /ˈbɒtld/ (adj)
certainly /ˈsɜːtnli/ (adv)
choose /tʃuːz/ (v)
coconut /ˈkəʊkənʌt/ (n)
cost /kɒst/ (v)
dessert /dɪˈzɜːt/ (n)
dish /dɪʃ/ (n)
forget /fəˈget/ (v)
fried /fraɪd/ (adj)
fry /fraɪ/ (v)
garlic bread /ˈgɑːlɪk bred/ (n)
grill /grɪl/ (v)
grilled /grɪld/ (adj)
helpful /ˈhelpfəl/ (adj)
homemade /ˌhəʊmˈmeɪd/ (adj)
location /ləʊˈkeɪʃən/ (n)
main course /ˌmeɪn ˈkɔːs/ (n)
miss /mɪs/ (v)
occasion /əˈkeɪʒən/ (n)
order /ˈɔːdə/ (n)
order /ˈɔːdə/ (v)
recommendation /ˌrekəmenˈdeɪʃən/ (n)
roast /rəʊst/ (adj)
roast /rəʊst/ (v)
service /ˈsɜːvɪs/ (n)
side dish /ˈsaɪd dɪʃ/ (n)
sparkling /ˈspɑːklɪŋ/ (adj)
spicy /ˈspaɪsi/ (adj)
starter /ˈstɑːtə/ (n)
steak /steɪk/ (n)
still /stɪl/ (adj)
superb /suːˈpɜːb/ (adj)
tasty /ˈteɪsti/ (adj)

Culture 7

add /æd/ (v)
baking powder /ˈbeɪkɪŋ ˌpaʊdə/ (n)
beat /biːt/ (v)
cut /kʌt/ (v)
frying pan /ˈfraɪɪŋ pæn/ (n)
grate /greɪt/ (v)
instructions /ɪnˈstrʌkʃənz/ (pl n)
mix /mɪks/ (v)
peel /piːl/ (v)
pot /pɒt/ (n)
recipe /ˈresɪpi/ (n)
repeat /rɪˈpiːt/ (v)
season /ˈsiːzən/ (v)

squeeze /skwiːz/ (v)
towel /ˈtaʊəl/ (n)
traditional /trəˈdɪʃənəl/ (adj)

Unit 8 – New places, new faces

8a

along /əˈlɒŋ/ (adv)
boring /ˈbɔːrɪŋ/ (adj)
bright /braɪt/ (adj)
cheap /tʃiːp/ (adj)
clean /kliːn/ (adj)
crowded /ˈkraʊdɪd/ (adj)
delicious /dɪˈlɪʃəs/ (adj)
dirty /ˈdɜːti/ (adj)
exciting /ɪkˈsaɪtɪŋ/ (adj)
expensive /ɪkˈspensɪv/ (adj)
fascinating /ˈfæsɪneɪtɪŋ/ (adj)
fashionable /ˈfæʃənəbəl/ (adj)
footprint /ˈfʊtprɪnt/ (n)
handprint /ˈhændprɪnt/ (n)
home to /ˈhəʊm tə/ (n)
interesting /ˈɪntrəstɪŋ/ (adj)
memorable /ˈmemərəbəl/ (adj)
modern /ˈmɒdn/ (adj)
nightlife /ˈnaɪtlaɪf/ (n)
noisy /ˈnɔɪzi/ (adj)
old /əʊld/ (adj)
outdoor /ˈaʊtdɔː/ (adj)
place /pleɪs/ (n)
polluted /pəˈluːtɪd/ (pp)
quiet /ˈkwaɪət/ (adj)
ride /raɪd/ (n)
sight /saɪt/ (n)
stall /stɔːl/ (n)
star /stɑː/ (n)
suit everyone's wallet (phr)
tasty /ˈteɪsti/ (adj)
trendy /ˈtrendi/ (adj)
unforgettable /ʌnfəˈgetəbəl/ (adj)

8b

comfortable /ˈkʌmftəbəl/ (adj)
destination /ˌdestɪˈneɪʃən/ (n)
dry /draɪ/ (adj)
foreign /ˈfɒrən/ (adj)
noisy /ˈnɔɪzi/ (adj)
peaceful /ˈpiːsfəl/ (adj)
popular with /ˈpɒpjʊlə wɪð/ (adj)
quiet /ˈkwaɪət/ (adj)
safe /seɪf/ (adj)

8c

aquarium /əˈkweəriəm/ (n)
art gallery /ˈɑːt ˌgæləri/ (n)
buy souvenirs (phr)
fancy /ˈfænsi/ (v)
feel like doing sth (phr)
gift shop /ˈgɪft ʃɒp/ (n)
go for a walk (phr)
go on rides (phr)
historic /hɪˈstɒrɪk/ (adj)
hotspot /ˈhɒtspɒt/ (n)
market /ˈmɑːkɪt/ (n)
museum /mjuːˈziəm/ (n)
park /pɑːk/ (n)
pay a visit (phr)
restaurant /ˈrestərɒnt/ (n)
sandy /ˈsændi/ (adj)
see paintings (phr)
see statues (phr)
sports stadium /ˈspɔːts ˌsteɪdiəm/ (n)
theatre /ˈθɪətə/ (n)
theme park /ˈθiːm pɑːk/ (n)
traditional /trəˈdɪʃənəl/ (adj)
trendy /ˈtrendi/ (adj)
try local dishes (phr)
watch a football match (phr)
watch a performance (phr)
website /ˈwebsaɪt/ (n)

Culture 8

boat cruise /ˈbəʊt kruːz/ (n)
fjord /fiːɔːd/ (n)
kayaking /ˈkaɪækɪŋ/ (n)
mountain biking /ˈmaʊntɪn ˌbaɪkɪŋ/ (n)
must-see /ˈmʌst siː/ (n)
trekking /ˈtrekɪŋ/ (n)
volcano /vɒlˈkeɪnəʊ/ (n)
waterfall /ˈwɔːtəfɔːl/ (n)
welcome /ˈwelkəm/ (v)

Unit 9 – Times change

9a

airport /ˈeəpɔːt/ (n)
coast /kəʊst/ (n)
donkey /ˈdɒŋki/ (n)
electricity /ɪˌlekˈtrɪsəti/ (n)
feature /ˈfiːtʃə/ (n)
ferry boat /ˈferi bəʊt/ (n)
fishing boat /ˈfɪʃɪŋ bəʊt/ (n)
get around /ˌget əˈraʊnd/ (phr v)
guest house /ˈgest haʊs/ (n)

islander /ˈaɪləndə/ (n)
reach /riːtʃ/ (v)
running water /ˌrʌnɪŋ ˈwɔːtə/ (n)
seem /siːm/ (v)
stone cottage /ˈstəʊn ˌkɒtɪdʒ/ (n)

9b

afford /əˈfɔːd/ (v)
ancient /ˈeɪnʃənt/ (adj)
board game /ˈbɔːd geɪm/ (n)
brick /brɪk/ (n)
carpet /ˈkɑːpɪt/ (n)
century /ˈsentʃəri/ (n)
civilisation /ˌsɪvəlaɪˈzeɪʃən/ (n)
controlled /kənˈtrəʊld/ (adj)
corn /kɔːn/ (n)
count /kaʊnt/ (v)
explorer /ɪkˈsplɔːrə/ (n)
feast /fiːst/ (n)
flat-screen /ˈflæt skriːn/ (adj)
horrible /ˈhɒrəbəl/ (adj)
hunting /ˈhʌntɪŋ/ (n)
narrow /ˈnærəʊ/ (adj)
poor /pɔː/ (adj)
porridge /ˈpɒrɪdʒ/ (n)
powered /ˈpaʊəd/ (adj)
public bath /ˌpʌblɪk ˈbɑːθ/ (n)
quinoa /ˈkiːnwɑː/ (n)
rich /rɪtʃ/ (adj)
slave /sleɪv/ (n)
steering wheel /ˈstɪərɪŋ wiːl/ (n)
transportation /ˌtrænspɔːˈteɪʃən/ (n)
underground /ˌʌndəˈgraʊnd/ (adj)
wheel /wiːl/ (n)
wooden /ˈwʊdn/ (adj)

9c

bank /bæŋk/ (n)
bridge /brɪdʒ/ (n)
bus station /ˈbʌs ˌsteɪʃən/ (n)
café /ˈkæfeɪ/ (n)
cinema /ˈsɪnəmə/ (n)
department store /dɪˈpɑːtmənt stɔː/ (n)
destination /ˌdestɪˈneɪʃən/ (n)
direction /dəˈrekʃən/ (n)
fire station /ˈfaɪə ˌsteɪʃən/ (n)
head /hed/ (v)
hospital /ˈhɒspɪtəl/ (n)
hotel /həʊˈtel/ (n)
international /ˌɪntəˈnæʃənəl/ (adj)
museum /mjuːˈziəm/ (n)
park /pɑːk/ (n)
petrol station /ˈpetrəl ˌsteɪʃən/ (n)

police station /pəˈliːs ˌsteɪʃən/ (n)
port /pɔːt/ (n)
post office /ˈpəʊst ˌɒfɪs/ (n)
restaurant /ˈrestərɒnt/ (n)
school /skuːl/ (n)
straight /streɪt/ (adv)
supermarket /ˈsuːpəmɑːkɪt/ (n)
train station /treɪn ˌsteɪʃən/ (n)
warehouse /ˈweəhaʊs/ (n)

Culture 9

butcher /ˈbʊtʃə/ (n)
chicken /ˈtʃɪkɪn/ (n)
describe /dɪˈskraɪb/ (v)
for sale /fə ˈseɪl/ (prep phr)
honour /ˈɒnə/ (v)
poultry /ˈpəʊltri/ (pl n)
row /rəʊ/ (n)
royal /ˈrɔɪəl/ (adj)
strange /streɪndʒ/ (adj)

Values C: Respect

beach /biːtʃ/ (n)
common /ˈkɒmən/ (adj)
cost /kɒst/ (v)
cover /ˈkʌvə/ (v)
culture /ˈkʌltʃə/ (n)
dress code /dres kəʊd/ (n)
endangered species /ɪnˌdeɪndʒəd ˈspiːʃiːz/ (n)
enter /ˈentə/ (v)
hiking trail /ˈhaɪkɪŋ ˌtreɪl/ (n)
insult /ɪnˈsʌlt/ (v)
leave /liːv/ (v)
local /ˈləʊkəl/ (adj)
locals /ˈləʊkəlz/ (pl n)
product /ˈprɒdʌkt/ (n)
research /rɪˈsɜːtʃ/ (v)
respect /rɪˈspekt/ (v)
rubbish /ˈrʌbɪʃ/ (n)
ruins /ˈruːɪnz/ (pl n)
take off /teɪk ˈɒf/ (phr v)
temple /ˈtempəl/ (n)
tip /tɪp/ (n)
top /tɒp/ (adj)

Public Speaking Skills

block /blɒk/ (n)
bottom /ˈbɒtəm/ (n)
civilisation /ˌsɪvəlaɪˈzeɪʃən/ (n)
comment /ˈkɒment/ (n)
course /kɔːs/ (n)
draw /drɔː/ (n)
grow /grəʊ/ (v)
important /ɪmˈpɔːtənt/ (adj)

knowledge /ˈnɒlɪdʒ/ (n)
landmark /ˈlændmɑːk/ (n)
object /ˈɒbdʒɪkt/ (n)
origin /ˈɒrɪdʒɪn/ (n)
past /pɑːst/ (adj)
proud of /ˈpraʊd əv/ (adj)
purpose /ˈpɜːpəs/ (n)
root /ruːt/ (n)
start /stɑːt/ (n)
symbol /ˈsɪmbəl/ (n)
tomb /tuːm/ (n)
university /ˌjuːnɪˈvɜːsəti/ (n)
wide /waɪd/ (adj)
wonder /ˈwʌndə/ (n)

Unit 10 – Their stories live on

10a

actor /ˈæktə/ (n)
amazing /əˈmeɪzɪŋ/ (adj)
career /kəˈrɪə/ (n)
cartoon /kɑːˈtuːn/ (n)
come up with /ˌkʌm ˈʌp wɪð/ (phr v)
company /ˈkʌmpəni/ (n)
crash /kræʃ/ (v)
decide /dɪˈsaɪd/ (v)
engineer /ˌendʒɪˈnɪə/ (n)
equation /ɪˈkweɪʒən/ (n)
film director /fɪlm dəˌrektə/ (n)
fire /faɪə/ (n)
inventor /ɪnˈventə/ (n)
lawyer /ˈlɔːjə/ (n)
lead to /ˈliːd tə/ (v)
look into /lʊk ɪntə/ (phr v)
luck /lʌk/ (n)
model /ˈmɒdl/ (n)
offer /ˈɒfə/ (v)
original /əˈrɪdʒɪnəl/ (adj)
painter /ˈpeɪntə/ (n)
physicist /ˈfɪzɪsɪst/ (n)
politician /ˌpɒləˈtɪʃən/ (n)
produce /prəˈdjuːs/ (v)
robbery /ˈrɒbəri/ (n)
self-portrait /ˌself ˈpɔːtrət/ (n)
teacher /ˈtiːtʃə/ (n)
theory of relativity /ˈθɪəri əv ˌreləˈtɪvəti/ (n)
tool /tuːl/ (n)
zoologist /zəʊˈɒlədʒɪst/ (n)

10b

abroad /əˈbrɔːd/ (adv)
academic /ˌækəˈdemɪk/ (adj)

army /ˈɑːmi/ (n)
bury /ˈberi/ (v)
die /daɪ/ (v)
discover /dɪsˈkʌvə/ (v)
fight /faɪt/ (v)
join /dʒɔɪn/ (v)
lend /lend/ (v)
medicine /ˈmedsən/ (n)
Nobel Prize /ˌnəʊbel ˈpraɪz/ (n)
penicillin /ˌpenəˈsɪlɪn/ (n)
post /pəʊst/ (v)
professor /prəˈfesə/ (n)
raise /reɪz/ (v)
receive /rɪˈsiːv/ (v)
scientist /ˈsaɪəntɪst/ (n)
social media profile /ˌsəʊʃəl ˈmiːdɪə ˌprəʊfaɪl/ (n)
unfortunately /ʌnˈfɔːtʃənətli/ (adv)
update /ˈʌpdeɪt/ (v)

10c

attract sb's attention (phr)
bark /bɑːk/ (v)
confused /kənˈfjuːzd/ (adj)
cry /kraɪ/ (n)
dive into /daɪv ɪntə/ (v)
engine /ˈendʒɪn/ (n)
entrance /ˈentrəns/ (n)
excited /ɪkˈsaɪtɪd/ (adj)
flame /fleɪm/ (n)
frightened /ˈfraɪtnd/ (adj)
grab /græb/ (v)
guess /ges/ (v)
happy /ˈhæpi/ (adj)
headphones /ˈhedfəʊnz/ (pl n)
inch /ɪntʃ/ (n)
nanny /ˈnæni/ (n)
negative /ˈnegətɪv/ (adj)
pale /peɪl/ (adj)
perseverance /ˌpɜːsɪˈvɪərəns/ (n)
positive /ˈpɒzətɪv/ (adj)
proud /praʊd/ (adj)
ranger /ˈreɪndʒə/ (n)
save /seɪv/ (v)
scare /skeə/ (v)
selfie /ˈselfi/ (n)
shocked /ʃɒkt/ (adj)
shore /ʃɔː/ (n)
thank /θæŋk/ (v)
truck /trʌk/ (n)
upset /ʌpˈset/ (adj)
wave /weɪv/ (v)
whiz /wɪz/ (v)
worried /ˈwʌrid/ (adj)

Culture 10

care for sb /keə fə/ (phr v)
childhood /ˈtʃaɪldhʊd/ (n)
common /ˈkɒmən/ (adj)
definitely /ˈdefɪnətli/ (adv)
fame /feɪm/ (n)
forever /fərˈevə/ (adv)
inspire /ɪnˈspaɪə/ (v)
join /dʒɔɪn/ (v)
leather /ˈleðə/ (n)
peaceful /ˈpiːsfəl/ (adj)
true /truː/ (adj)

Unit 11 – Time will tell

11a

cause /kɔːz/ (v)
charity /ˈtʃærəti/ (n)
disappear /ˌdɪsəˈpɪə/ (v)
electric car /ɪˌlektrɪk ˈkɑː/ (n)
end up /ˌend ˈʌp/ (phr v)
environmental club /ɪnˌvaɪrənˌmentl ˈklʌb/ (n)
miserable /ˈmɪzərəbəl/ (adj)
packaging /ˈpækɪdʒɪŋ/ (n)
plant /plɑːnt/ (v)
pollution /pəˈluːʃən/ (n)
rainforest /ˈreɪnfɒrɪst/ (n)
recycle /ˌriːˈsaɪkəl/ (v)
rubbish /ˈrʌbɪʃ/ (n)
save /seɪv/ (v)
smart /smɑːt/ (adj)
turn off /ˌtɜːn ˈɒf/ (phr v)
wild animal /ˌwaɪld ˈænɪməl/ (n)

11b

attend /əˈtend/ (v)
breathe /briːð/ (v)
department /dɪˈpɑːtmənt/ (n)
fire brigade /faɪə brɪˌgeɪd/ (n)
flying car /ˈflaɪɪŋ ˈkɑː/ (n)
oxygen mask /ˈɒksɪdʒən mɑːsk/ (n)
pill /pɪl/ (n)
presentation /ˌprezənˈteɪʃən/ (n)
protect /prəˈtekt/ (v)
race /reɪs/ (n)
underwater /ˌʌndəˈwɔːtə/ (adj)
vet /vet/ (n)
win /wɪn/ (v)

Word List

11c

animal sanctuary /ˈænɪməl ˌsæŋktʃuəri/ (n)
course /kɔːs/ (n)
hiking /ˈhaɪkɪŋ/ (n)
introduce /ˌɪntrəˈdjuːs/ (v)
land /lænd/ (v)
move house (phr)
part-time /ˌpɑːt ˈtaɪm/ (adv)
term /tɜːm/ (n)
volunteer /ˌvɒlənˈtɪə/ (v)
windsurfing /ˈwɪndsɜːfɪŋ/ (n)

Culture 11

application form /ˌæplɪˈkeɪʃən ˌfɔːm/ (n)
branch /brɑːntʃ/ (n)
cruelty /ˈkruːəlti/ (n)
fill out /ˌfɪl ˈaʊt/ (phr v)
form /fɔːm/ (v)
in common /ɪn ˈkɒmən/ (prep phr)
interview /ˈɪntəvjuː/ (n)
prevention /prɪˈvenʃən/ (n)
rescue /ˈreskjuː/ (v)
training course /ˈtreɪnɪŋ kɔːs/ (n)
volunteer /ˌvɒlənˈtɪə/ (n)

Unit 12 – Take a break

12a

ancient temple /ˌeɪnʃənt ˈtempəl/ (n)
crowded /ˈkraʊdɪd/ (adj)
disgusting /dɪsˈɡʌstɪŋ/ (adj)

empty /ˈempti/ (adj)
exhibit /ɪɡˈzɪbɪt/ (n)
handmade /ˌhændˈmeɪd/ (adj)
horrible /ˈhɒrəbəl/ (adj)
modern /ˈmɒdn/ (adj)
noisy /ˈnɔɪzi/ (adj)
palace /ˈpæləs/ (n)
quiet /ˈkwaɪət/ (adj)
spices /ˈspaɪsɪz/ (pl n)
try /traɪ/ (v)

12b

couscous /ˈkʊskʊs/ (n)
cycle /ˈsaɪkəl/ (v)
explore /ɪkˈsplɔː/ (v)
island /ˈaɪlənd/ (n)
lake /leɪk/ (n)
ocean /ˈəʊʃən/ (n)

12c

acceptance /əkˈseptəns/ (n)
bottom /ˈbɒtəm/ (n)
desert /ˈdezət/ (n)
dolphin /ˈdɒlfɪn/ (n)
go canoeing (phr)
go ice skating (phr)
go on a helicopter tour (phr)
go snorkelling (phr)
medieval /ˌmediˈiːvəl/ (adj)
post /pəʊst/ (n)
sandboarding /ˈsændbɔːdɪŋ/ (n)
statue /ˈstætʃuː/ (n)
suggestion /səˈdʒestʃən/ (n)
swim /swɪm/ (v)

Culture 12

adventure /ədˈventʃə/ (n)
canoe /kəˈnuː/ (v)
come true (phr)
frozen /ˈfrəʊzən/ (adj)
further /ˈfɜːðə/ (adv)
imagine /ɪˈmædʒɪn/ (v)
nature lover /ˈneɪtʃə ˌlʌvə/ (n)
on offer /ɒn ˈɒfə/ (prep phr)
package holiday /ˈpækɪdʒ ˌhɒlədeɪ/ (n)
promise /ˈprɒmɪs/ (v)
sail /seɪl/ (v)
totem pole /ˈtəʊtəm pəʊl/ (n)
trip /trɪp/ (n)

Values D: Environmental awareness

awareness /əˈweənəs/ (n)
can /kæn/ (n)
challenging /ˈtʃælɪndʒɪŋ/ (adj)
clean energy /ˌkliːn ˈenədʒi/ (n)
cool /kuːl/ (adj)
cycle lane /ˈsaɪkəl leɪn/ (n)
electronics /ˌelɪkˈtrɒnɪks/ (n)
encourage /ɪnˈkʌrɪdʒ/ (v)
environmental /ɪnˌvaɪrənˈmentl/ (adj)
lung /lʌŋ/ (n)
nowadays /ˈnaʊədeɪz/ (adv)
on foot /ɒn ˈfʊt/ (prep phr)
pedestrian-only street /pəˈdestriən əʊnli ˌstriːt/ (n)
pollution /pəˈluːʃən/ (n)
public /ˈpʌblɪk/ (adj)

public transport /ˌpʌblɪk ˈtrænspɔːt/ (n)
recycling programme /riːˈsaɪklɪŋ ˌprəʊɡræm/ (n)
relaxing /rɪˈlæksɪŋ/ (adj)
save /seɪv/ (v)
set up /ˌset ˈʌp/ (phr v)
solar power /ˌsəʊlə ˈpaʊə/ (n)
space /speɪs/ (n)
waste /weɪst/ (n)
wind power /ˈwɪnd ˌpaʊə/ (n)

Public Speaking Skills

audience /ˈɔːdiəns/ (n)
capital /ˈkæpɪtl/ (n)
celebrate /ˈseləbreɪt/ (v)
connect /kəˈnekt/ (v)
digital /ˈdɪdʒɪtl/ (adj)
e-waste /ˈiː weɪst/ (n)
educational /ˌedjuˈkeɪʃənəl/ (adj)
factory /ˈfæktəri/ (n)
follow /ˈfɒləʊ/ (v)
mode /ˈmɒdl/ (n)
nature reserve /ˈneɪtʃə rɪˌzɜːv/ (n)
network /ˈnetwɜːk/ (n)
nickname /ˈnɪkneɪm/ (n)
provide /prəˈvaɪd/ (v)
rare /reə/ (adj)
recycling bin /riːˈsaɪklɪŋ bɪn/ (n)
representative /ˌreprɪˈzentətɪv/ (n)
transport /ˈtrænspɔːt/ (n)

Irregular Verbs

Infinitive	Past	Past Participle	Infinitive	Past	Past Participle
be /biː/	was /wɒz/	been /biːn/	learn /lɜːn/	learnt (learned) /lɜːnt (lɜːnd)/	learnt (learned) /lɜːnt (lɜːnd)/
bear /beə/	bore /bɔː/	born(e) /bɔːn/	leave /liːv/	left /left/	left /left/
beat /biːt/	beat /biːt/	beaten /ˈbiːtən/	lend /lend/	lent /lent/	lent /lent/
become /brˈkʌm/	became /brˈkeɪm/	become /brˈkʌm/	let /let/	let /let/	let /let/
begin /brˈgɪn/	began /brˈgæn/	begun /brˈgʌn/	lie /laɪ/	lay /leɪ/	lain /leɪn/
bite /baɪt/	bit /bɪt/	bitten /ˈbɪtən/	light /laɪt/	lit /lɪt/	lit /lɪt/
blow /bləʊ/	blew /bluː/	blown /bləʊn/	lose /luːz/	lost /lɒst/	lost /lɒst/
break /breɪk/	broke /brəʊk/	broken /ˈbrəʊkən/	make /meɪk/	made /meɪd/	made /meɪd/
bring /brɪŋ/	brought /brɔːt/	brought /brɔːt/	mean /miːn/	meant /ment/	meant /ment/
build /bɪld/	built /bɪlt/	built /bɪlt/	meet /miːt/	met /met/	met /met/
burn /bɜːn/	burnt (burned) /bɜːnt (bɜːnd)/	burnt (burned) /bɜːnt (bɜːnd)/	pay /peɪ/	paid /peɪd/	paid /peɪd/
burst /bɜːst/	burst /bɜːst/	burst /bɜːst/	put /pʊt/	put /pʊt/	put /pʊt/
buy /baɪ/	bought /bɔːt/	bought /bɔːt/	read /riːd/	read /red/	read /red/
can /kæn/	could /kʊd/	(been able to /bɪn ˈeɪbəl tə/)	ride /raɪd/	rode /rəʊd/	ridden /ˈrɪdən/
catch /kætʃ/	caught /kɔːt/	caught /kɔːt/	ring /rɪŋ/	rang /ræŋ/	rung /rʌŋ/
choose /tʃuːz/	chose /tʃəʊz/	chosen /ˈtʃəʊzən/	rise /raɪz/	rose /rəʊz/	risen /ˈrɪzən/
come /kʌm/	came /keɪm/	come /kʌm/	run /rʌn/	ran /ræn/	run /rʌn/
cost /kɒst/	cost /kɒst/	cost /kɒst/	say /seɪ/	said /sed/	said /sed/
cut /kʌt/	cut /kʌt/	cut /kʌt/	see /siː/	saw /sɔː/	seen /siːn/
deal /diːl/	dealt /delt/	dealt /delt/	sell /sel/	sold /səʊld/	sold /səʊld/
dig /dɪg/	dug /dʌg/	dug /dʌg/	send /send/	sent /sent/	sent /sent/
do /duː/	did /dɪd/	done /dʌn/	set /set/	set /set/	set /set/
draw /drɔː/	drew /druː/	drawn /drɔːn/	sew /səʊ/	sewed /səʊd/	sewn /səʊn/
dream /driːm/	dreamt (dreamed) /dremt (driːmd)/	dreamt (dreamed) /dremt (driːmd)/	shake /ʃeɪk/	shook /ʃʊk/	shaken /ˈʃeɪkən/
drink /drɪŋk/	drank /dræŋk/	drunk /drʌŋk/	shine /ʃaɪn/	shone /ʃɒn/	shone /ʃɒn/
drive /draɪv/	drove /drəʊv/	driven /ˈdrɪvən/	shoot /ʃuːt/	shot /ʃɒt/	shot /ʃɒt/
eat /iːt/	ate /eɪt/	eaten /ˈiːtən/	show /ʃəʊ/	showed /ʃəʊd/	shown /ʃəʊn/
fall /fɔːl/	fell /fel/	fallen /ˈfɔːlən/	shut /ʃʌt/	shut /ʃʌt/	shut /ʃʌt/
feed /fiːd/	fed /fed/	fed /fed/	sing /sɪŋ/	sang /sæŋ/	sung /sʌŋ/
feel /fiːl/	felt /felt/	felt /felt/	sit /sɪt/	sat /sæt/	sat /sæt/
fight /faɪt/	fought /fɔːt/	fought /fɔːt/	sleep /sliːp/	slept /slept/	slept /slept/
find /faɪnd/	found /faʊnd/	found /faʊnd/	smell /smel/	smelt (smelled) /smelt (smeld)/	smelt (smelled) /smelt (smeld)/
fly /flaɪ/	flew /fluː/	flown /fləʊn/	speak /spiːk/	spoke /spəʊk/	spoken /ˈspəʊkən/
forbid /fəˈbɪd/	forbade /fəˈbeɪd/	forbidden /fəˈbɪdən/	spell /spel/	spelt (spelled) /spelt (speld)/	spelt (spelled) /spelt (speld)/
forget /fəˈget/	forgot /fəˈgɒt/	forgotten /fəˈgɒtən/	spend /spend/	spent /spent/	spent /spent/
forgive /fəˈgɪv/	forgave /fəˈgeɪv/	forgiven /fəˈgɪvən/	stand /stænd/	stood /stʊd/	stood /stʊd/
freeze /friːz/	froze /frəʊz/	frozen /ˈfrəʊzən/	steal /stiːl/	stole /stəʊl/	stolen /ˈstəʊlən/
get /get/	got /gɒt/	got /gɒt/	stick /stɪk/	stuck /stʌk/	stuck /stʌk/
give /gɪv/	gave /geɪv/	given /ˈgɪvən/	sting /stɪŋ/	stung /stʌŋ/	stung /stʌŋ/
go /gəʊ/	went /went/	gone /gɒn/	swear /sweə/	swore /swɔː/	sworn /swɔːn/
grow /grəʊ/	grew /gruː/	grown /grəʊn/	sweep /swiːp/	swept /swept/	swept /swept/
hang /hæŋ/	hung (hanged) /hʌŋ (hæŋd)/	hung (hanged) /hʌŋ (hæŋd)/	swim /swɪm/	swam /swæm/	swum /swʌm/
have /hæv/	had /hæd/	had /hæd/	take /teɪk/	took /tʊk/	taken /ˈteɪkən/
hear /hɪə/	heard /hɜːd/	heard /hɜːd/	teach /tiːtʃ/	taught /tɔːt/	taught /tɔːt/
hide /haɪd/	hid /hɪd/	hidden /ˈhɪdən/	tear /teə/	tore /tɔː/	torn /tɔːn/
hit /hɪt/	hit /hɪt/	hit /hɪt/	tell /tel/	told /təʊld/	told /təʊld/
hold /həʊld/	held /held/	held /held/	think /θɪŋk/	thought /θɔːt/	thought /θɔːt/
hurt /hɜːt/	hurt /hɜːt/	hurt /hɜːt/	throw /θrəʊ/	threw /θruː/	thrown /θrəʊn/
keep /kiːp/	kept /kept/	kept /kept/	understand /ˌʌndəˈstænd/	understood /ˌʌndəˈstʊd/	understood /ˌʌndəˈstʊd/
know /nəʊ/	knew /njuː/	known /nəʊn/	wake /weɪk/	woke /wəʊk/	woken /ˈwəʊkən/
lay /leɪ/	laid /leɪd/	laid /leɪd/	wear /weə/	wore /wɔː/	worn /wɔːn/
lead /liːd/	led /led/	led /led/	win /wɪn/	won /wʌn/	won /wʌn/
			write /raɪt/	wrote /rəʊt/	written /ˈrɪtən/